Summer Fun for Kids

A Parent's Guide to Indoor and Outdoor
Activities
for Kids Aged 6–12

Erin Campbell Wilson

Table of Contents

Introduction

Summer means happy times and good sunshine. It means going to the beach, going to Disneyland, having fun. –Brian Wilson

Welcome to *Summer Fun for Kids*, a book dedicated to helping parents and caregivers create an unforgettable summer filled with joy, adventure, and cherished memories. This book aims to set the tone of friendly, fun, and choice-driven activities that allow parents to tailor their summer plans to fit their unique family dynamic. None of the suggestions provided is written in stone, as parents are encouraged to adapt and expand them to suit their individual preferences. So, let's embark on a journey of exploration and imagination, making this a summer your children will remember for years to come.

The Purpose of This Book

The purpose of this book is to serve as a resource for parents seeking to keep their children active, engaged, and entertained during the summer months. By offering a wide range of exciting and age-appropriate activities, I aim to give parents the tools they need to make the most of this valuable time spent with their kids. Summer presents an opportunity for children to have new experiences, ignite their curiosity, and strengthen family bonds, and this book is designed to facilitate just that.

Why Keep Kids Active During Summer?

The benefits of keeping children active during the summer are numerous and far-reaching (activecamps, 2024). First and foremost, physical activity promotes good health and well-being. Summertime provides the perfect opportunity for children to enjoy outdoor games, sports, and exploration, boosting their overall fitness levels. Additionally, staying active helps prevent the consequences of a sedentary lifestyle, such as obesity and related health issues.

Moreover, engaging in various activities during summer nurtures a child's sense of discovery and sparks their imagination. Kids can explore their creativity and expand their horizons, whether it's a nature scavenger hunt, building a fort, or even experimenting with different arts and crafts projects. These experiences build cognitive growth, problem-solving skills, and a love for learning.

Equally important, summer activities provide an opportunity for families to spend quality time together. By participating in these shared adventures, parents and children create lasting memories, strengthen their relationships, and build a foundation of trust and understanding that will serve them well.

What's Included?

This book offers various activities, ensuring there's something for every child's interest and age group. There are endless possibilities for summer fun, from outdoor adventures like camping and picnics to creative pursuits such as art projects and cooking experiments. I have also included suggestions for indoor and outdoor activities, allowing parents to plan accordingly regardless of the weather or their surroundings.

How to Use This Book

I understand that every child is unique and has different interests and abilities. Therefore, I have provided some tips to help parents select and modify activities appropriately for each child's age and developmental stage. You will also find that most of the materials needed for these activities can easily be found at home or the local store, ensuring that the cost doesn't deter you.

While engrossed in summer fun, safety is of the utmost importance. I have outlined some general safety considerations and precautions to ensure that every activity is conducted securely and with supervision.

In each activity section, you will find a list of required materials and suggested preparations to help parents clearly understand what they need to gather and set up beforehand. This will help ease the planning process and ensure a smooth execution of each activity.

Remember, there is no right way to enjoy summer. This book serves as a starting point, but parents are encouraged to tailor the activities to fit their family's interests, location, and available time. Feel free to modify, substitute, or combine activities as needed to create a meaningful and enjoyable summer for your unique family dynamic.

Making the Most of Summer

Summer is a cherished time that passes by all too quickly. By using this book as a guide, parents can make the most of this precious time with their children, creating memories that will last a lifetime. From simple moments of laughter to grand adventures, these summer experiences will undoubtedly be treasured and spoken of for years.

This book addresses the pain point faced by parents of young children who desire to entertain, engage, and stimulate their kids during the summer. I understand the delicate balance between avoiding the feeling of extended school time and not having a complete free-for-all. This book offers a variety of activities that strike that balance, ensuring an enjoyable and enriching summer for the whole family.

As an author with personal health and wellness coaching experience and the mother of young adults, I have gathered insights from my professional and personal life to curate this collection of activities. Drawing from outdoor adventures on my acreage, family travels, and my involvement as an active 4-H leader, I bring a wealth of practical knowledge that parents can benefit from.

By the end of this book, you will feel equipped with a gem of a resource for planning your summer adventures. From selecting activities to understanding age appropriateness and gathering required materials, you'll gain the confidence to create a summer experience that everyone in your family can enjoy. Let's make this summer one to remember!

Chapter 1:

Outdoor Adventures

Restore balance. Most kids have technology, school and extracurricular activities covered. It's time to add a pinch of adventure, a sprinkle of sunshine and a big handful of outdoor play. –Penny Whitehouse

Join us as we embark on an exciting journey into the great outdoors, a world filled with endless possibilities and fun-filled adventures that are perfect for families with children. Discover the wonders of nature as we invite you to break free from the routine and explore the beauty that surrounds us.

As you wake up to a world of new experiences and thrilling escapades, we encourage families to embrace the joy of discovery and immerse themselves in nature's wonders. This chapter isn't just an invitation—it's a call to ignite the spirit of exploration and create lasting memories in the great outdoors.

Explore the captivating activities that await you outside, from nature hunts to exciting water play. Every family can find their own adventure, no matter where they live or how limited their resources may be.

This chapter aims to help families looking to add a touch of nature's magic to their everyday lives. It celebrates the special connection between families and the outdoors, offering endless opportunities for shared happiness, exploration, and excitement (Fatima, 2024). So, gather your loved ones, and let's create unforgettable moments together.

Nature Hunts

Nature hunts present a wonderful opportunity for children to immerse themselves in the beauty of the outdoors while having a great time. This engaging activity not only develops a sense of exploration but also provides valuable learning experiences that can deepen their connection with the natural world. Here are some components that can enhance the enjoyment and educational value of nature hunts for children.

Scavenger Hunts

Organizing a scavenger hunt adds an element of excitement and adventure to the nature exploration experience. Children are motivated to venture into their surroundings and discover hidden treasures waiting to be found. Parents or caregivers can create a list of items for the children to seek out, ranging from specific types of leaves, rocks, or flowers to more elusive elements like animal tracks or nests. This not only encourages kids to observe their environment closely but also instills in them a sense of wonder and curiosity about the diversity of nature around them.

Bug and Plant Identification

Integrating bug and plant identification into the nature hunt elevates the activity to a valuable learning opportunity. By encouraging children to observe and identify various bugs, insects, and plant species, they not only enhance their knowledge of local flora and fauna but also develop a deeper appreciation for the intricate ecosystems that surround them. Engaging in bug and plant identification builds a sense of environmental awareness and encourages children to view the natural world with a curious and inquisitive mindset.

Through participatory and educational experiences like nature hunts, children can not only enjoy the outdoors but also cultivate a sense of stewardship and respect for the environment. By immersing themselves in the wonders of the natural world, kids can foster a lifelong love for nature and develop an understanding of the interconnectedness of all living beings. Nature hunts offer endless opportunities for exploration, discovery, and learning, making them a truly enriching summer activity for children of all ages.

Pro Tip

As you engage in nature hunts with your kids, take the time to discuss their findings and encourage them to ask questions about the natural elements they encounter. Consider creating a nature journal where they can document their observations and discoveries, further enhancing their learning experience and creating a lasting record of their outdoor adventures.

Water Play

Water play stands out as a dynamic and immersive experience that not only entertains children but also cultivates essential physical, social, and developmental skills. Supervision and safety considerations are paramount to ensure a secure and enjoyable environment for all participants. Here are some innovative water-play ideas that promise hours of fun-filled entertainment and learning for kids:

DIY Water Park

Transforming your backyard or a local park into a DIY water park offers a paradise of aquatic enjoyment for children of all ages. Setting up water sprinklers, inflatable pools, and waterslides creates a vibrant water wonderland where kids can cool off, splash around, and revel in the joys of summer. Introducing water toys like water guns or water cannons enhances the interactive experience, allowing for creativity and imaginative play in a refreshing outdoor setting.

Water Balloon Games

Water balloon games inject a dose of excitement and laughter into hot summer days. Children can engage in a variety of entertaining activities, including water balloon toss, relays, and even water balloon piñatas. These games not only boost hand-eye coordination and teamwork skills but also provide a refreshing escape from the heat, encouraging active participation and camaraderie among players.

DIY Waterslide Fun

Setting up a DIY waterslide introduces a thrilling element of adventure to the water play repertoire. Kids can glide down a water-soaked chute, relishing the exhilarating sensation of speed and sliding. Creating a DIY waterslide is a simple yet effective endeavor, requiring only plastic sheets, water, and a touch of soap to facilitate smooth gliding. This activity promotes physical activity, coordination, and balance while offering a splendid opportunity for children to cool off and embrace the carefree spirit of summertime.

When engaging in water play activities with your children, prioritize safety measures such as supervision, proper hydration, and sun protection to ensure a secure and enjoyable experience. Encourage kids to explore, experiment, and immerse themselves in the joys of water play, developing an appreciation for physical fitness, social interaction, and a lifelong love of active lifestyles.

Pro Tip

Incorporate elements of learning and environmental awareness into water play by discussing topics like water conservation, aquatic habitats, or the importance of staying hydrated. Encourage children to appreciate and respect water as a precious resource, instilling values of responsibility and sustainability from a young age.

Sports and Games

Engaging in sports and games during the summer provides kids with numerous benefits, including physical exercise, the promotion of teamwork, communication, and sportsmanship. However, it's crucial to prioritize safety and supervision to prevent injuries. Here are some engaging activities for kids during the summer:

Backyard Soccer and Baseball

Playing soccer or baseball in the backyard is an excellent way for kids to refine their sports skills, stay active, and enjoy quality time with friends and family. To ensure safety, clear the playing area of any hazards, and consider using softer balls to minimize the risk of injury.

Pro Tip

Consider setting up mini-tournaments or friendly competitions to keep kids motivated and engaged.

Relay Races

Organizing relay races can be both thrilling and competitive for kids, promoting teamwork, coordination, and physical fitness. You can create various relay-race themes to add excitement and encourage participation.

Pro Tip

Incorporate fun challenges or obstacles into the races to make them more engaging and challenging.

Capture the Flag

This classic outdoor game involves strategy, teamwork, and physical activity. It encourages critical thinking, communication, and problem-solving skills while providing an entertaining and energetic outlet for kids.

Pro Tip

Create zones or designated areas to add more depth and strategy to the game, making it more captivating for the kids.

Outdoor Swimming Lessons

Swimming lessons in the summer not only offer a fun activity but also an essential skill for water safety. Learning to swim outdoors can help kids build confidence in the water while enjoying the benefits of physical activity.

Pro Tip

Encourage kids to participate in pool games or challenges after their swimming lessons to reinforce their newly acquired skills and make the experience more enjoyable.

Exploration and Discovery

Exploration and discovery activities offer children the opportunity to immerse themselves in the natural world, sparking curiosity and nurturing a deeper connection to their surroundings. Here are further details on the activities mentioned:

Geocaching

Geocaching is a modern-day treasure-hunt app that blends technology with outdoor exploration. Participants use GPS coordinates to locate hidden containers, known as caches, in various outdoor locations. Geocaching not only encourages teamwork and problem-solving skills but also creates a sense of adventure and discovery. Children develop spatial awareness, critical-thinking, and navigation skills while exploring new environments and discovering hidden gems.

Nature Hikes and Trail Exploration

Nature hikes and trail exploration provide children with the chance to engage their senses and discover the wonders of the natural world. As they explore different terrains, kids can learn about local flora and fauna, observe wildlife, and gain a deeper appreciation for the environment. These activities offer opportunities for physical exercise, mindfulness, and bonding with family and friends while helping to develop an understanding of conservation and ecosystem diversity.

Birdwatching and Wildlife Journaling

Birdwatching offers children a glimpse into the fascinating world of avian species and wildlife. By observing birds in their natural habitats, kids can enhance their knowledge of biodiversity, ecology, and animal behaviors. Keeping a wildlife journal allows young enthusiasts to document their observations, draw sketches, and reflect on their encounters with nature. This practice promotes scientific inquiry, attention to detail, and environmental awareness while encouraging creativity and storytelling. If you're looking for apps that help identify birds, you can download the Audubon Bird Guide app. This free guide contains information about more than 800 North American bird species. This app helps identify birds and even helps track birds you've already seen.

Photography, Creating Books, Stories, and Albums

Introducing children to photography as a means of capturing their outdoor adventures can cultivate their observational skills and artistic expression. Encouraging kids to create photo books, stories, or digital albums featuring their nature experiences empowers them to share their perspectives and memories creatively. Through storytelling and visual representation, children can reflect on their outdoor journeys, convey emotions, and showcase their appreciation for the environment, creating a sense of stewardship and environmental advocacy.

Pro Tip

Consider incorporating interactive and educational elements into exploration and discovery activities by introducing nature-themed challenges, scavenger hunts, or identification games. This approach not only enhances the learning experience but also encourages active participation and engagement, making the outdoor adventures even more enriching and enjoyable for children.

Creative Outdoor Fun

Engaging in creative outdoor activities provides children with a multifaceted experience that goes beyond mere entertainment. These activities not only encourage imaginative thinking and artistic expression but also help to build a deep appreciation for nature and the outdoors. Here's an in-depth exploration of creative outdoor activities:

Chalk Art Murals

Chalk art murals offer children an open canvas to express their creativity and imagination. Whether they're drawing lively scenes, intricate patterns, or imaginative designs, the temporary nature of chalk art allows kids to experiment and unleash their artistic talents in an outdoor setting.

This activity provides an outlet for self-expression; encourages collaboration among friends and siblings; and adds vibrant, ephemeral artwork to outdoor spaces, creating a sense of community and creativity.

Building Fairy Houses

Constructing fairy houses amid natural surroundings ignites a sense of wonder and magic in children. By using found objects such as twigs, leaves, and flowers, kids can craft miniature dwellings for fictional creatures, blending storytelling, imaginative play, and hands-on creativity. This activity not only encourages a deeper connection with nature but also promotes resourcefulness, environmental appreciation, and a sense of whimsy as children envision the magical inhabitants of their carefully crafted fairy abodes.

Garden Planting Projects

Engaging in garden planting projects not only introduces children to the world of horticulture and botany but also instills valuable lessons about nurturing and sustaining the environment. Through hands-on experiences in planting flowers, vegetables, or herbs, kids gain insight into plant life cycles, soil health, and the importance of caring for living organisms. Gardening projects create a sense of responsibility and accomplishment as children witness the fruits of their labor and develop a deeper understanding of the interconnectedness between humans and nature.

Picnicking

A traditional outdoor activity, picnicking offers children an opportunity to enjoy the simple pleasures of nature and community. Involving kids in the preparation and setup of a picnic helps them develop a sense of responsibility and teamwork while elevating the experience to be more than just a meal outdoors. It encourages mindfulness and relaxation, promotes family bonding, and cultivates a sense of appreciation for natural landscapes and outdoor camaraderie.

Movie in the Backyard/Park

Hosting a movie night under the open sky adds a touch of enchantment and novelty to the outdoor experience for kids. By transforming an outdoor space into a makeshift cinematic venue, children can relish the thrill of watching their favorite films in a unique setting, helping them develop a sense of imagination and relaxation while strengthening their connection to the outdoors.

Pro Tip

Encourage children to combine different creative outdoor activities to create a holistic and enriching experience. For example, they can start the day with a nature hike to gather materials for a fairy house, engage in chalk art murals in the afternoon, followed by a garden planting project. This integration allows kids to explore diverse forms of creativity, learn from their outdoor adventures, and make meaningful connections between artistic expression and nature appreciation, resulting in a more immersive and fulfilling outdoor experience.

Turning our focus from outdoor exploration to indoor creativity, we now embark on a journey into the whimsical world of creative crafts. In Chapter 2, we will unearth a treasure trove of imaginative projects, artful endeavors, and hands-on activities that will inspire young minds to unleash their creativity and bring their artistic visions to life.

Chapter 2:

Creative Crafts

Don't think about making art, just get it done. Let everyone else decide if it's good or bad, whether they love it or hate it. While they are deciding, make even more art.
–Andy Warhol

Imagine a summer filled with the delightful sounds of children's laughter, the rhythmic swish of paintbrushes, and the clinking of colorful beads coming together to form a symphony of creativity. That is the essence of what awaits within this chapter. It is a vibrant, joyous celebration of childhood wonder, where hands are transformed into tools of artistic expression and everyday materials become the building blocks for imaginative exploration.

The essence of this chapter lies in the celebration of creativity, the spirit of exploration, and the sheer delight that comes from creating something unique and personal. It is designed to captivate the minds of children and provide them with craft projects that are not only entertaining but also educational, building vital skills such as problem-solving, dexterity, and cognitive development. This chapter aims to be the go-to resource for parents and caregivers seeking to infuse summer days with artful, engaging, and delightful activities for the kids.

This chapter is an all-encompassing guide, offering an array of craft ideas that promise to mesmerize, captivate, and inspire younger audiences. From classic projects to modern twists on traditional crafts, the offerings within these pages seek to cater to a wide spectrum of interests and preferences (Gautieri & Thomas, 2024). Whether your child is an aspiring artist, an avid inventor, or a curious explorer, there is a creative venture waiting to be discovered.

Join us on this exploratory voyage through the world of crafting, where the summer fun knows no bounds, and the creative spirit flows freely. Within these pages, you will find an abundance of crafting adventures tailored to entertain, educate, and enchant. From traditional favorites to innovative new concepts, this chapter promises some fun activities.

Art Projects

Here are some details on a few engaging art activities for kids during the summer.

Painting With Natural Brushes

Encouraging kids to use natural materials as painting tools can be an enriching and creative experience. Using items such as leaves, twigs, feathers, or flowers as brushes builds a deeper connection with nature, as it allows children to engage with the textures and shapes of different natural objects, enhancing their sensory exploration of the world around them.

One of the exciting aspects of painting with natural brushes is the opportunity to inspire creativity through experimentation. As children utilize various natural materials to create different strokes and patterns, they are prompted to think outside the box and explore the unique properties of each item. For example, a leaf might produce a delicate, wispy stroke, while a twig could create bold, textured lines. This process not only nurtures their imagination but also helps them develop a deeper understanding of the textures and forms found in nature.

Furthermore, painting with natural brushes serves as an educational opportunity for kids to learn about the environment and sustainability. It emphasizes the beauty and versatility of natural materials, instilling a sense of appreciation and respect for the resources provided by the natural world. This activity opens up conversations about the importance of conservation and the impact of our choices on the environment, creating a mindset of environmental stewardship in young minds.

Through this art activity, children can create a wide range of artwork, from abstract designs to nature-inspired scenes, using natural brushes. This hands-on experience not only encourages artistic expression but also helps them develop fine motor skills and artistic abilities as they learn to manipulate and control the natural tools to bring their visions to life on canvas or paper.

Pro Tip

To enhance the experience of painting with natural brushes, encourage children to collect their own materials from nature. Take them on a nature walk or explore the backyard together, showing them the various textures and shapes of leaves, twigs, flowers, and other natural objects that can be used as brushes. This hands-on approach not only strengthens their connection with the natural world but also makes the painting process even more personal and meaningful. Additionally, provide a variety of paint colors and surfaces (such as canvas, paper, or rocks) to inspire endless artistic possibilities and encourage experimentation with different combinations of natural brushes and paint mediums.

Rock Painting

Rock painting offers numerous benefits for kids, particularly in terms of emotional and artistic development. The act of painting on rocks can serve as a therapeutic and calming activity, allowing children to engage in a creative process that helps them develop self-expression. It also promotes mindfulness and relaxation as they concentrate and focus on painting intricate designs on the rocks.

Furthermore, the act of decorating rocks with vibrant colors and unique patterns can significantly boost children's self-esteem and confidence. When kids see the finished product, they experience a sense of accomplishment and pride in creating something aesthetically pleasing with their own hands. This positive reinforcement can be influential in building their self-worth and creative abilities.

Additionally, rock painting can be a social activity that encourages interaction and sharing among kids. By exchanging painted rocks with friends or family members, children can develop relationships and collaboration, thus creating a sense of camaraderie and connection within their community.

Moreover, displaying painted rocks in various outdoor spaces, such as gardens, parks, or public areas, can have a meaningful impact. It not only contributes to the beautification of these spaces but also spreads joy and positivity to those who encounter them. This act of sharing their art with others can instill a sense of accomplishment and purpose in children, as they realize the impact their creativity can have on the world around them.

Pro Tip

When rock painting, start with a light base layer of paint before adding intricate designs or details. This will help to create a smoother surface for the designs, and the colors will be more vibrant and stand out. It is also helpful to let each layer of paint dry completely before adding additional layers or details to prevent smudging or smearing.

DIY Tie-Dye

Tie-dyeing is a highly versatile activity that allows children to explore their artistic side while engaging in a hands-on and interactive process. The experience of tie-dyeing introduces kids to the world of colors and patterns, stimulating their creativity and imagination.

One of the key benefits of tie-dyeing is that it encourages experimentation with different dyeing techniques. Children can explore various folding methods, such as spiral, accordion, or crumple, to create different patterns and designs on the fabric. This process of decision-making and problem-solving enables kids to learn and develop their critical-thinking skills.

Additionally, tie-dyeing is a messy, yet enjoyable, activity that can bring joy and laughter to children. From mixing the dyes to the process of applying them to the fabric, kids can immerse themselves in the sensory experience of seeing the vibrant colors unfold before their eyes. The element of surprise when unwrapping the dyed fabrics after they have been set adds an exciting anticipation to the creative process.

One of the perks of tie-dyeing is that the finished projects can be used in a practical way. Children can proudly wear their personalized tie-dyed clothes, showcasing their unique and individual designs, which allows them to express their personality and creativity through wearable art. Alternatively, the dyed fabrics can be used as decorative items, such as wall hangings or pillow covers, adding a pop of color and personality to their living spaces.

Overall, tie-dyeing offers children a fun and creative outlet to explore the world of colors, patterns, and self-expression. It nurtures their artistic abilities, develops their decision-making skills, and allows them to create unique and personal works of art.

Pro Tip

One useful tip for tie-dyeing is to prewash the fabric before dyeing it to remove any sizing or finishes that could prevent the dye from penetrating the fabric evenly. It's also helpful to wear gloves and aprons to protect clothing and skin from any stains or mess. When applying the dye, make sure to saturate the fabric thoroughly to ensure vibrant, full coverage results and consider using a dye fixative to set the color and prevent it from washing out over time.

Crafting With Recyclables

Crafting with recyclables is another amazing way to engage. Let's explore some fantastic crafts in more detail.

Bottle Cap Art

Bottle cap art is a creative and eco-friendly craft that encourages children to repurpose materials and reduce waste. By collecting plastic bottle caps from various beverages, kids have the opportunity to transform these seemingly ordinary objects into colorful and imaginative creations.

One of the benefits of bottle cap art is that it nurtures children's creativity and imagination. They can experiment with different shapes, sizes, and colors of bottle caps to create unique designs. It challenges them to think outside the box and find innovative ways to arrange the caps into patterns or pictures. This process stimulates their problem-solving skills as they figure out how best to utilize the caps and create visually appealing artwork.

Not only is bottle cap art a creative outlet, but it can also be quite functional. Kids can use their artistic skills to make practical items such as magnets, coasters, or even mosaic-style artworks using bottle caps. This multitasking aspect of bottle cap art not only allows children to express their creativity but also provides them with personalized and useful pieces that can be used or displayed in their homes or given as gifts.

Engaging in bottle cap art also teaches kids about the importance of upcycling and repurposing materials. Through this craft, they become more aware of environmental issues and the impact of waste on the planet. By showcasing how everyday items like bottle caps can be transformed into beautiful art, kids learn the value of recycling and resourcefulness. This can lead to the development of eco-conscious habits as they actively seek out ways to repurpose materials in their everyday lives.

Pro Tip

Sort and organize your bottle caps by color, size, or design before starting a project. This can make it easier to plan out your artwork and create cohesive designs. Additionally, consider using a strong adhesive when attaching the bottle caps to your chosen surface to ensure that your artwork remains intact and durable.

Cardboard Castles

Building cardboard castles is a fun and engaging DIY project that encourages children to unleash their creativity and imagination. By repurposing cardboard boxes, tubes, and other recyclable materials, kids can embark on a magical castle-building adventure, creating their own whimsical kingdom filled with towers, turrets, and drawbridges.

One of the key benefits of constructing cardboard castles is that it promotes hands-on construction skills among children. They can practice measuring, cutting, and assembling pieces to bring their castle structures to life. This process not only enhances their fine motor skills but also gives them a sense of accomplishment and pride as they see their creations take shape. Additionally, if multiple children work together on a castle-building project, it encourages teamwork, collaboration, and communication skills as they pool their ideas and resources to construct a grand castle together.

The act of decorating the cardboard castles is a creative adventure that allows kids to personalize their creations. They can use paint, markers, glitter, and other embellishments to add colorful details and designs to their castles. From designing intricate flags and royal banners to crafting miniature furniture for the castle interiors, children can infuse their personalities and imaginations into every aspect of their creations, making each castle truly unique and special.

Beyond the construction and decoration process, cardboard castles offer endless opportunities for imaginative play and storytelling. Once the castles are complete, children can immerse themselves in a world of knights, princesses, dragons, and magical adventures. This imaginative play not only entertains kids but also stimulates their cognitive and social development, encouraging them to create stories, scenarios, and characters within the enchanted setting of their cardboard castle.

In essence, building cardboard castles is a fantastic DIY project that combines creativity, construction skills, and imaginative play in a magical and collaborative setting. It allows children to explore their creativity, work together, and engage in immersive storytelling adventures within the walls of their own imaginative kingdoms.

Pro Tip

One good way to start building cardboard castles is to create a design or blueprint to help guide your construction. You can draw out your castle design on paper, including measurements and labels for each piece, or use online tutorials and templates for inspiration. This will help ensure that your castle structure is sturdy and balanced and that you have all the necessary cardboard pieces before getting started. Additionally, consider using a hot glue gun or sturdy tape to secure the cardboard pieces in place for a more durable castle structure.

Newspaper Hats

Making newspaper hats is a delightful eco-friendly craft that provides children with an opportunity to repurpose old newspapers into fashionable and imaginative headwear. By learning basic origami or various paper-folding techniques, kids can explore a range of hat styles, from classic sailor hats to whimsical party hats, using simple and readily available materials.

One of the key advantages of making newspaper hats is that it is a budget-friendly and sustainable way for kids to engage with design and fashion concepts. It encourages creativity as children experiment with different folding methods, shapes, and decorative elements to craft their own unique hats, allowing them to express their individual style and personality. By using recyclable materials, kids also begin to understand the value of repurposing and reducing waste while creating fun and fashionable accessories.

Designing and wearing newspaper hats can spark imaginative play and inspire role-playing scenarios. Children can immerse themselves in creative storytelling as they pretend to be pirates, explorers, or even newspaper reporters, adding an interactive and playful element to the crafting experience. This imaginative play not only entertains kids but also stimulates their cognitive and social development, encouraging them to create scenarios and characters within the context of their newly crafted hats.

In addition to being a creative accessory, newspaper hats offer a sustainable alternative to disposable party hats or costumes. By showcasing how simple materials can be transformed into wearable art pieces, kids learn about the potential of everyday items to be repurposed and transformed into unique, eco-friendly creations. In doing so, children gain an awareness of sustainable practices and the significance of making environmentally conscious choices in their creative endeavors.

Pro Tip

To enhance the creativity and learning experience for kids while making newspaper hats, consider incorporating educational elements into the activity. You can share interesting facts about the history of hats, introduce cultural significance of various hat styles, or discuss the environmental impact of upcycling materials. By combining hands-on crafting with educational insights, children can develop a deeper appreciation for sustainability, design, and fashion.

Nature-Inspired Crafts

Nature-inspired crafts help bring the outdoors inside and capture children in a creative and interactive way. Here are some fun activities to try.

Pinecone Animals

Pinecone animals are a popular craft activity that involves transforming simple natural objects—in this case, pinecones—into imaginative creatures using paint, glue, and other craft materials. This activity not only allows children to explore nature's textures, shapes, and colors but also promotes hand-eye coordination and fine motor skills as they manipulate the materials.

One of the main benefits of creating pinecone animals is that it encourages children to use their imagination and creativity. By envisioning their animal designs and bringing them to life through crafting, children have the opportunity to express their unique ideas and create something truly original. This process of making decisions and solving problems, such as how to attach various materials to the pinecone or how to create specific animal features, enhances their problem-solving skills and boosts their critical-thinking abilities.

Moreover, through making pinecone animals, children can acquire knowledge about different animals and their unique characteristics. This craft can be an opportunity to introduce various animal species and discuss their habitats, behaviors, and other interesting facts. By researching and incorporating these details into their creations, children not only expand their animal knowledge but also engage in a multidisciplinary learning experience that combines science, art, and natural exploration.

Displaying pinecone animals as decorative items can provide children with a sense of accomplishment and pride. Seeing their artwork showcased in their living spaces or in outdoor areas can boost their self-confidence and motivate them to continue exploring their creative talents. Furthermore, the addition of pinecone animals as decor adds a natural, organic touch to the ambiance and aesthetics of the space, bringing a sense of earthiness and connection to nature.

Pro Tip

To make pinecone animals even more engaging and educational, consider using this craft as a starting point for a broader exploration of nature. You can encourage children to seek out different types of pinecones and other natural materials, such as leaves or twigs, and create their own unique creatures. Additionally, you can prompt discussions about the importance of preserving natural habitats and the impact of human activity on the environment. By exploring these topics, children can develop a deeper understanding of the natural world and learn to appreciate the beauty and diversity of nature around them.

Leaf Rubbings

Leaf rubbings are a creative and educational activity that involves using leaves as natural templates to create textured and detailed artworks by laying the leaves under paper and rubbing crayons or other media over the surface. This technique provides children with a hands-on opportunity to explore the varied textures, shapes, and patterns found in nature, while also promoting the development of fine motor skills as they engage in the rubbing process.

Creating leaf rubbings can help a child develop a deeper appreciation and awareness of the beauty and diversity of the natural world. By observing and comparing the shapes, sizes, and textures of different leaves, children not only enhance their observational skills but also gain insight into the unique characteristics of various plant species. Through this interactive exploration, they develop a sense of connection to nature and an understanding of the intricate details present in their environment.

Furthermore, leaf rubbings can serve as a catalyst for creative expression and storytelling. The patterns and textures produced through leaf rubbings can inspire children's imaginations, prompting them to invent stories or characters based on the leaf designs. This creative exercise encourages children to think critically, make imaginative connections, and express themselves through art, fostering their overall creativity and cognitive skills.

Once completed, leaf-rubbing artworks can be utilized in various ways, such as framing them as decorative pieces, turning them into greeting cards, bookmarks, or even incorporating them into collages. This versatile nature of leaf rubbings not only provides children with an opportunity to showcase their artwork but also offers a low-cost and eco-friendly means of creating unique and personal gifts or decor items. By incorporating these nature-inspired creations into indoor spaces, children can bring a touch of the outdoors inside, enhancing the aesthetic appeal of their surroundings and creating a deeper connection with the natural world around them.

Pro Tip

To add an extra dimension to leaf rubbings, encourage children to experiment with different types of leaves, including those with unique shapes, sizes, and textures. Additionally, suggest mixing up the mediums used for rubbing, such as colored pencils, pastels, or even watercolor paints, to create diverse and vibrant leaf-rubbing artworks. This experimentation not only enhances the creative process but also allows children to explore the endless possibilities of leaf rubbings and discover new ways to express themselves artistically.

Shell Mosaics

Creating shell mosaics is a fun and engaging activity that involves arranging seashells in various designs or patterns on surfaces such as cardboard, paper, or even rocks. This craft provides children with an opportunity to explore the different shapes, colors, and textures of seashells, promoting the development of observational and tactile skills.

Through creating shell mosaics, children can experiment with arranging the shells in different ways to create visually appealing designs. This artistic process enables them to explore concepts such as color harmonies, composition, and spatial awareness. Through trial and error, children develop an understanding of how to manipulate the shells to create various effects, ultimately resulting in a unique work of art that showcases their creativity and artistic skills.

In addition to providing an artistic outlet, shell mosaics give children an educational opportunity to learn about marine animals and their habitats. Creating shell mosaics also provides an opportunity for parents or teachers to start a conversation about the natural environment and to promote conservation awareness. This activity could serve as a platform to discuss various issues surrounding coastal ecosystems such as overfishing, pollution, or ocean acidification.

Displaying shell mosaics is an excellent way to add a natural, beachy touch to living spaces and invite the beauty of the ocean into indoor environments. Framing the shell mosaics and displaying them on the wall or including them in a beach-themed gallery adds a personal touch to the decor and creates a unique visual appeal to the space.

Pro Tip

When creating shell mosaics, encourage children to mix and match different types and sizes of seashells to add depth and visual interest to their designs. Additionally, consider incorporating other natural elements such as sand, pebbles, or sea glass to enhance the overall aesthetic and create a diverse and textured mosaic artwork. This approach expands the creative possibilities and allows children to experiment with various materials to create unique and dynamic compositions that capture the essence of the ocean environment.

DIY Toys and Games

DIY activities offer a creative way for kids to enjoy summer while helping them develop their imagination, problem-solving skills, and resourcefulness. Let's dive into a few easy DIY activities.

Homemade Kites

Making homemade kites is a fun and rewarding activity that combines crafting and outdoor play. Using various materials such as paper, dowels, string, and ribbons, children can develop their own unique kite designs, promoting the development of fine motor skills and enhancing their creativity.

Designing and building kites offers a hands-on learning experience about aerodynamics, physics, and weather conditions. Through making kites, children can experiment with the elements that affect flight, such as lift, drag, and wind patterns, gaining a deeper understanding of scientific concepts in a practical and engaging way. This knowledge can spark a fascination with science and inspire children to pursue interests that align with their newfound understanding of physics and other scientific principles.

Flying homemade kites encourages outdoor exploration and physical activity. It provides an opportunity for kids to enjoy fresh air, sunshine, and the thrill of seeing their creations take flight. With the encouragement to run with their kites to launch it, children gain the benefits of physical activity, such as developing gross motor skills and burning off energy.

This DIY activity can also be an invitation for family or community kite-flying events, promoting social interaction and bonding as everyone participates in the excitement of flying their homemade kites. Children can collaborate on their kite-making process and work together to launch their creations, fostering a sense of camaraderie and teamwork. Building and flying kites is an excellent way for children from diverse backgrounds to work together, regardless of their age or skill level, promoting inclusion and developing relationships.

To make homemade kites, you will need some basic materials such as paper, dowels, string, ribbons, scissors, glue, and decorative materials such as markers, stickers, or paint. The process of making kites is straightforward and accessible, with various online resources and tutorials available to guide children through the crafting process, supporting them every step of the way.

Pro Tip

Use tissue paper or thin plastic bags instead of heavier paper for your kite to make it lighter, more aerodynamic, and easier to fly. Also, make sure to choose open spaces such as parks or beaches with steady wind currents for flying your kite while keeping away from any obstacles such as buildings or trees. Finally, ensure that you put a long tail on your kite to provide stability and balance, helping it stay in flight longer.

Paper-Plate Frisbees

To make paper-plate frisbees, you will need a few materials:

- **Paper plates:** You can use regular paper plates, which are readily available at grocery stores or party supply stores. Choose plates that are sturdy enough to hold their shape when folded.

- **Decorations:** Get creative and decorate your paper plates with colors, drawings, or stickers of your choice. This step is optional but can make your frisbees more personalized and fun.

- **Scissors:** You'll need a pair of scissors to cut out the frisbee shape from the folded paper plate.

Steps to Make Paper-Plate Frisbees

1. **Take a paper plate and decorate it.** Use markers, crayons, or any other art supplies to decorate the paper plate. You can draw patterns, make designs, or even put stickers on it. Let your creativity run wild and make your frisbee unique.

2. **Fold the paper plate in half.** Once your decorating is complete and the plate is dry, fold it in half from the center. Make sure the edges of the plate line up with each other. Press along the fold to create a crease. This will help maintain the shape of your frisbee.

3. **Cut out a frisbee shape.** With the plate still folded, use scissors to cut out a triangular shape from the curved edges. The shape should resemble a classic frisbee shape. It's better to cut a larger shape than you think you need, as it can affect the flight of the frisbee.

4. **Unfold and play.** Finally, gently unfold the paper plate and admire your paper-plate frisbee. The triangular cut-out will create an open space in the middle of the plate, allowing it to fly through the air when thrown. Now it's time to have some

fun! Take your newly made paper-plate frisbee outside and start throwing it around with friends or family.

Making paper-plate frisbees is a simple, fun activity that people of all ages can enjoy. It encourages creativity, as you get to decorate the frisbee yourself. It also promotes physical activity, as you can play with it outdoors and get moving. Additionally, making paper-plate frisbees can introduce basic scientific concepts such as aerodynamics and flight dynamics as you observe how the frisbee moves through the air.

Pro Tip

Before decorating and cutting the paper plate to make a frisbee, consider reinforcing the edges with clear tape or laminating the paper plate. This extra step can help increase the durability of the frisbee, making it last longer and withstand more throws and catches.

DIY Board Games

Creating DIY board games is a fantastic way to engage children in a creative and educational activity that can provide hours of entertainment. Here's a look at the benefits and steps involved in making DIY board games.

Benefits of DIY Board Games

- **Creativity and critical thinking:** Designing their own board games allows children to unleash their creativity by coming up with unique game concepts, themes, and rules. They also exercise critical-thinking skills as they design challenges and gameplay mechanics.

- **Social interaction:** DIY board games provide an opportunity for kids to involve siblings, friends, or family members in playing their creations. This builds social interaction, teamwork, communication, and healthy competition.

- **Educational value:** Through the process of creating and playing board games, children develop strategic thinking, decision-making skills, and logical reasoning. They learn to follow rules, set objectives, and understand game dynamics, all of which are valuable life skills.

- **Patience and adaptability:** The iterative process of designing and testing board games teaches children about patience, resilience, and adaptability. They learn to embrace both success and challenges, making adjustments to improve their games based on feedback and experience.

Steps to Make DIY Board Games

1. **Design the game.** Start by brainstorming ideas for your board game. Decide on a theme, objectives, and rules. Sketch a layout for the game board and outline how players will progress and win.

2. **Gather materials.** Collect the necessary materials, such as cardboard or a board for the game board, craft materials like paper and scissors for creating components, markers or paint for decorating, playing pieces such as buttons or small toys, and dice or cards for gameplay.

3. **Create the game board.** Use the cardboard or board to create the game board. Design and decorate the board with markers or paint to match your game's theme. Add spaces, paths, or sections to navigate during gameplay.

4. **Make playing pieces and components.** Craft playing pieces such as buttons, coins, or mini-toys that represent the players. Create cards with instructions or actions that players draw during the game. Design dice with symbols or numbers for movement or decision-making.

5. **Establish rules and gameplay.** Develop clear rules for how the game is played, including how players move, win, lose, and

interact with one another. Define objectives, challenges, and any special mechanics unique to your game.

6. **Test and refine.** Playtest your DIY board game with friends or family members to identify any issues, confusion, or areas for improvement. Adjust the rules, components, or gameplay based on feedback and your observations.

7. **Play and have fun.** Once your DIY board game is finalized, gather players to enjoy the game you've created. Encourage strategic thinking, cooperation, and friendly competition among participants.

Pro Tip

Encourage children to document their game-design process by keeping a game-design notebook or journal. This allows them to jot down ideas, sketch game layouts, note rule variations, and track feedback from playtesting sessions. Keeping a record of their game-creation journey can help them reflect on their progress, refine their ideas, and enhance their game-design skills over time.

Creating Journals, Making Storybooks, and Crafting Puppets for Plays

Crafting journals, storybooks, and puppets provides children with a wonderful opportunity to engage in expressive and imaginative activities that can enhance various skills. Here's a comprehensive exploration of the benefits and steps involved in crafting these creative items:

Benefits of Crafting Journals, Storybooks, and Puppets

- **Literacy skills development:** Engaging in writing, drawing, and storytelling develops literacy skills as children practice expressing their ideas and emotions through words and art. This can help strengthen their vocabulary, sentence structure, and overall communication abilities.

- **Self-expression:** Crafting journals, storybooks, and puppets offers children a means to express their thoughts, feelings, and creativity. This can contribute to their emotional development, self-awareness, and confidence in sharing their perspectives and stories.

- **Narrative development:** Creating storybooks allows children to develop narrative skills as they invent characters, plot lines, and settings for their stories. They can explore storytelling techniques, such as plot development, dialogue, and descriptive language, which can enhance their writing and storytelling abilities.

- **Artistic exploration:** Crafting puppets provides an opportunity for children to explore different materials, textures, and construction techniques. This can stimulate their creativity and understanding of visual arts as they design and bring their puppet characters to life.

Steps to Craft Journals, Storybooks, and Puppets

1. **Creating journals**

    o   Start by choosing a blank notebook or set of papers to create a journal.

    o   Decorate the cover and pages with drawing materials such as colored pencils, pens, markers, stickers, ribbons, or glitter to personalize the journal.

    o   Encourage children to fill the pages with their thoughts, reflections, drawings, or stories.

2. **Making storybooks**

    o   Encourage children to develop a story idea, including characters, settings, and a plot.

    o   Have them write and illustrate their stories on blank paper or in a customized storybook format.

- Consider creating a cover and dedicating a space for the author's name and any illustrations that complement the story.

3. **Designing and crafting puppets**

- Provide construction paper or other materials to create the puppet characters, allowing children to cut, shape, and assemble them.

- Use drawing materials and decorative materials to add details and features to the puppets.

- Encourage children to develop puppet plays by creating scenarios, dialogues, and performances with their puppet characters.

4. **Creative expression and play**

- Encourage children to use their journals, storybooks, and puppets as tools for creative expression and imaginative play.

- Provide opportunities for them to share their stories, perform puppet shows, and engage in collaborative storytelling activities with friends or family members.

Pro Tip

Encourage children to create puppet shows based on the stories written in their storybooks, using the puppets to act out scenes from their favorite books, or incorporating their journals into storytelling activities. Integrating these elements allows for a holistic creative experience, where children can combine writing, visual arts, and performance for a richer, more immersive creative playtime.

Now that we've explored some creative crafting adventures, let's turn our attention to the world of indoor games. When unexpected events put outdoor adventures on hold, it's the perfect time to discover indoor games. From innovative game ideas to fascinating scientific experiments,

Chapter 3 introduces you to a few activities to ignite young minds and provide endless entertainment.

Chapter 3:

Indoor Rainy-Day Games and

Discovery

Our challenge isn't so much to teach children about the natural world, but to find ways to sustain the instinctive connections they already carry. –Terry Krautwurst

As a parent, there are days when the unexpected arrival of rainy weather or uninviting coldness may confine both you and your child indoors. In such instances, the challenge becomes finding ways to keep your child engaged and entertained, while also promoting learning and creativity. This chapter tackles this predicament, offering a variety of engaging and educational activities for keeping kids entertained while stuck indoors. It aims to provide parents with a range of options for turning indoor days into opportunities for fun and exploration (Sager, 2023).

Classic Indoor Games

There are plenty of classic indoor games that can add excitement and fun to a rainy day. Here are a few examples:

- **Hide-and-seek:** Hide-and-seek is a timeless game that can be enjoyed by children of all ages. It is a simple yet exhilarating game where one person hides while others close their eyes and count. The seekers then try to find the hidden person. This game not only keeps children active and engaged but also encourages problem-solving and critical thinking as they search for the best hiding spots.

- **Simon Says:** Simon Says is another classic game that can be played indoors on a rainy day. It challenges children to listen carefully and follow instructions. One person acts as "Simon" and gives commands, prefaced with the phrase "Simon says." The other players must follow the commands *only* if Simon says so. This game helps develop listening skills, enhances concentration, and promotes coordination.

- **Musical chairs:** Musical chairs is a popular game that can be played indoors, providing an opportunity to burn off energy while having loads of fun. Arrange chairs in a circle, with one less chair than the number of players. When the music plays, children walk around the chairs. When the music stops, they must quickly find a seat. The person left standing is out, and one more chair is removed. The game continues until there is only one player left. Musical chairs encourages activity, social interaction, and strategic thinking.

- **DIY craft session:** Set up a DIY craft station with various art supplies such as colored paper, markers, glue, scissors, and stickers. Encourage children to unleash their creativity by making paper crafts, cards, or even simple origami creations. This activity not only engages children in hands-on art projects but also allows them to express themselves through different mediums.

- **Storytelling circle:** Create a cozy storytelling circle with pillows or blankets and encourage children to take turns narrating bedtime stories, creating imaginative tales, or retelling their favorite fables. This activity not only sparks children's creativity and language skills but also builds a sense of camaraderie and shared storytelling experience.

- **Indoor scavenger hunt:** Design an indoor scavenger hunt by hiding small items or clues around the house for children to find. You can customize the hunt based on educational themes, such as colors, shapes, or letters, to make it both entertaining and educational. Indoor scavenger hunts promote teamwork, observation skills, and problem-solving abilities.

- **Dance party:** Host a mini–dance party in the living room by playing lively music and encouraging children to move and groove to the beat. Dancing not only provides a fun way to burn off energy but also enhances coordination, rhythm, and creativity. You can even introduce dance challenges or themed dance-offs to keep the party dynamic and engaging.

These fun indoor games are perfect for entertaining children on rainy days. They require minimal setup and can easily be adapted to different age groups. While these games have been played for generations, they never fail to captivate children and provide hours of enjoyment.

However, it's worth noting that these are just a few examples of classic indoor games. There are countless other games that can be explored, depending on the interests and preferences of the children. Innovative variations of these games can also be created to bring more excitement and uniqueness to the indoor playtime experience.

Puzzle and Brain Teasers

These are also great indoor activities to keep both kids and adults entertained on rainy summer days. Here are a few options to consider:

- **Jigsaw puzzles:** Jigsaw puzzles are a timeless indoor activity that can bring kids and adults together on rainy summer days. The beauty of jigsaw puzzles lies in their ability to cater to individuals of all ages with varying themes and levels of difficulty. Whether you prefer a challenging 1,000-piece landscape puzzle or a simpler animal-shaped puzzle for the little ones, there is a wide array of options to choose from. The process of assembling a jigsaw puzzle requires focus, patience, and problem-solving skills, making it an absorbing and gratifying pastime for all involved.

- **Sudoku and crosswords for kids:** Sudoku and crosswords provide an excellent opportunity for kids to engage their minds and boost their cognitive skills while having fun indoors. These brain-teasing puzzles are effective in enhancing logical reasoning, critical thinking, and problem-solving abilities in children. With specialized books and worksheets tailored for different age groups, age-appropriate challenges and themes can keep kids entertained and mentally stimulated for extended periods. Sudoku and crosswords not only entertain but also educate, offering a fun way for children to develop important skills.

- **DIY escape room:** For those seeking a more dynamic and immersive indoor activity, creating a DIY escape room is an exciting option that can captivate both kids and adults. Designing your own escape room involves planning and executing a series of puzzles, riddles, and clues strategically placed throughout your living space. Participants must work together to decipher the clues, unlock mysteries, and ultimately escape the room within a set time frame. This collaborative and interactive game encourages teamwork, problem-solving, and creativity, making it an entertaining and mentally stimulating experience for all participants.

Physical Activities

Engaging in physical activities is also a great way to stay active and have fun on rainy days. Here are some ideas to consider:

- **Indoor obstacle course:** Staying active on rainy days doesn't have to be a dampener on the fun. Setting up an indoor obstacle course is a great way to get your body moving and enjoy a bit of creative challenge at the same time. An obstacle course is easy to create with everyday items like pillows, chairs, and blankets to build a fun course that involves crawling, sliding, and balancing. Not only does this activity promote physical activity, but it also helps children develop problem-solving and planning skills. Creating a course that's challenging, yet manageable enough, helps to foster creativity and teamwork. It's an ideal indoor activity that keeps everyone engaged.

- **Build a pillow fort:** Building a pillow fort is a timeless indoor activity that encourages creativity and imagination. All you need are some blankets, pillows, and other materials to create a cozy and exciting hideaway. Younger kids will enjoy crawling into the fort and hiding amid the pillows and blankets, while older kids and adults might consider engaging in activities like board games or storytelling. The construction process is a hands-on project that promotes teamwork and planning skills while offering many opportunities for creative problem-solving. It's a great indoor activity that can provide hours of entertainment while keeping the mind and body active.

- **Dance party:** Hosting an indoor dance party is a fun way to get the body moving while lifting spirits in the process. You can make a playlist of upbeat tunes that everyone can dance to, or take turns choosing songs. It's a great way to release pent-up energy, de-stress, and improve overall mood. Dancing is an excellent exercise that enhances cardiovascular health, coordination, and balance. Making it a family affair ensures that everyone gets involved, and the indoor activity becomes an engaging team effort.

- **Balloon volleyball:** Balloon volleyball is a low-impact activity that can be played indoors. This game involves hitting a balloon back and forth across a makeshift "court" area, without the risk of breaking anything. This indoor activity requires little-to-no equipment, making it an accessible option for all ages. Balloon volleyball improves hand-eye coordination, agility, and teamwork, making it an ideal indoor activity to enjoy with friends and family. It's a low-stress game that everyone can play, making it an engaging and perfect pastime for rainy summer days.

Incorporating physical activities into your rainy-day routine can help you stay active, boost your mood, and create lasting memories with loved ones. Just because you're stuck inside doesn't mean you can't have a blast.

Board Games and Card Games

Traditional board games have stood the test of time as classic indoor entertainment for families. Games like Chutes and Ladders and Monopoly Junior offer young children a mix of luck, strategy, and interactive play that can keep them engaged for hours. These games not only provide fun but also help kids develop skills such as decision-making, counting, and following rules. Playing traditional board games with kids is a great way to bond as a family and create lasting memories on rainy days.

Simple DIY Board Games

For a creative and hands-on indoor activity, consider crafting DIY board games with your kids (see Chapter 2 for more on this). This activity allows children to design and personalize their own game boards, rules, and pieces, encouraging their creativity and imagination. Whether creating a simple race game or a memory challenge, DIY board games offer a unique and educational experience that encourages teamwork and problem-solving skills. Engaging in this creative process can be a fun and rewarding way to spend time indoors on a rainy day.

Card Game Variations

Card games provide a versatile option for indoor entertainment that can easily be customized to add variety and fun. Classic card games like Go Fish, Crazy Eights, or War can be modified with themed decks or special rules to create new gameplay experiences. These variations spark creativity, strategy, and excitement, making card games a flexible and engaging choice for indoor play. Whether playing with a standard deck of cards or a specialized set, exploring different variations of card games can keep the whole family entertained and challenged.

Family Game Night Ideas

Hosting a family game night is a wonderful way to strengthen bonds and create joyful memories together. The versatility of board games, card games, and group activities like charades or Pictionary allows for a diverse and engaging experience for everyone. Rotating through different games keeps the excitement alive and builds healthy competition while promoting teamwork and communication skills. Family game nights offer a perfect opportunity for quality time, laughter, and friendly rivalry, making them a cherished tradition for rainy days.

Book-Sharing and Verbal Create-a-Story

For a more relaxed and imaginative indoor activity, consider book-sharing or a verbal create-a-story game. Each participant can take turns sharing their favorite stories or contribute to a collaborative tale by adding a piece to the evolving narrative. This activity encourages creativity, verbal skills, and a love for storytelling, encouraging imagination and communication among participants. Book-sharing and verbal create-a-story games provide a low-key and enjoyable way to spend rainy days indoors, sparking inspiration and literary appreciation in a fun and engaging manner.

Indoor games can be a great way to have fun and stay entertained. Whether you're looking for physical activities, brain teasers, classic board games, or creative projects, there are plenty of options to choose from to keep you and your family engaged. But why limit children to just games?

When playing outside is not possible, science experiments can provide an engaging and educational way to pass the time. From simple investigations to more complex projects, there are plenty of ways to ignite your curiosity and build your knowledge of science, technology, engineering, and math (STEM) fields. Chapter 4 will explore various science experiments and activities for an immersive and fun learning experience for everyone.

Chapter 4:

Science Experiments and Exploration

Millions saw the apple fall, but Newton asked why. –Bernard Baruch

This chapter is all about igniting the spark of curiosity and encouraging kids to engage in hands-on, outdoor scientific activities. As the weather gets warmer and the days get longer, it's the perfect time for children to unleash their creativity and dive into the wonders of science right in their own backyard.

Let's look at a wide range of fun, safe, and educational science experiments that kids can conduct during the summer months. From creating erupting volcanoes to making slime, the opportunities for scientific exploration are endless (LaScala, 2020). We will provide step-by-step instructions, safety guidelines, and explanations of the scientific principles behind each experiment, making it enjoyable for kids of all ages.

Simple Experiments

Let's begin with a few simple experiments. These are fun learning activities that can keep your child busy and engaged for hours.

Volcano Eruption

Step-by-Step Instructions

1. Begin by constructing the volcano using a plastic bottle or paper-mâché. Ensure there is a cavity at the top to mimic a volcano cone.

2. Set up the volcano outdoors or on a protected surface like a table covered with plastic or newspapers to avoid making a mess.

3. Preparing the chemical mixtures:

   ○ In one container, combine 1/2 cup of white vinegar with a few drops of red food coloring to give it a lava-like appearance.

   ○ In another container, mix 1 tablespoon of baking soda with a few drops of dish soap. This will create the foaming effect during the eruption.

4. Place the baking soda mixture inside the cavity of the volcano where the eruption will originate.

5. Pour the vinegar mixture into the volcano cavity over the baking soda. Watch with amazement as the chemical reaction occurs, causing the foaming eruption that resembles lava flowing down the sides of the volcano.

Safety Guidelines

1. Make sure an adult is present to supervise the experiment from start to finish.

2. Perform the experiment indoors in a well-ventilated area to prevent inhaling the vinegar fumes.

3. Wear protective eyewear and gloves to safeguard against any accidental contact with the vinegar or baking soda mixture.

4. Keep the experiment away from flammable materials and open flames to prevent any accidents.

Scientific Explanation

The eruption of the volcano is a result of a chemical reaction between acetic acid (found in vinegar) and sodium bicarbonate (present in baking soda). When these two substances combine, they undergo an acid-base reaction. The acetic acid reacts with the sodium bicarbonate to produce carbon dioxide gas, water, and sodium acetate.

The carbon dioxide gas generated during the reaction builds up pressure inside the cavity, ultimately leading to the foaming eruption. The released foam resembles the lava flow of a real volcano, creating an exciting and visually captivating demonstration of chemical reactions in action. This experiment not only provides an engaging activity but also offers a valuable lesson in chemistry and scientific principles (*How to Make a Volcano: Step-by-Step Experiment*, 2024).

Rainbow in a Jar

Step-by-Step Instructions

- Begin by selecting a clear glass or clear plastic container for the experiment. Fill the container halfway with water, leaving enough space for the oil and food coloring.

- Slowly pour cooking oil into the container, allowing it to form a distinct layer on top of the water. Use caution to avoid spills and ensure the oil forms a uniform layer.

- Choose food coloring in colors that will create a rainbow effect, such as red, orange, yellow, green, blue, and purple. Add a few drops of each color into the container, aiming to distribute them in different areas.

- Observe as the food coloring droplets sink through the oil layer and disperse into the water below. The food coloring mixing with the water creates a mesmerizing rainbow-like effect.

Safety Guidelines

- Adult supervision is recommended throughout the experiment, especially when handling food coloring.

- Take care while handling food coloring to avoid staining clothes or skin. Wear protective gloves or apron, if necessary.

- Choose a suitable container that is strong and stable to avoid any accidents or breakages during the experiment.

Scientific Explanation

The creation of a rainbow in a jar relies on the principle of density. Oil is less dense than water, so when it is poured into the container, it forms a separate layer on top. Food coloring, being denser than oil, sinks through the oil layer until it reaches the water layer.

As the food coloring droplets enter the water, they disperse and mix with it. This phenomenon is known as *diffusion*, which occurs as the food coloring molecules move from an area of higher concentration (where it was initially dropped) to an area of lower concentration (the surrounding water).

The mixing of the food coloring with water creates a beautiful and vibrant rainbow-like effect. The different colors travel at different rates, resulting in streaks of color radiating from the original droplets. The end result is a stunning visual representation of the dispersion and diffusion of the food coloring in the water layer, resembling a magical rainbow in a jar.

Static Electricity Fun

Step-by-Step Instructions

1. Inflate a balloon and tie it securely.

2. Rub the balloon against a fabric surface such as a woolen sweater or a piece of fur. Rub it back and forth for about 30 seconds.

3. Slowly move the balloon close to small pieces of paper or a light object such as a light plastic straw.

4. Observe how the static electricity causes the paper or object to be attracted to the balloon, seemingly sticking to it.

5. Try rubbing the balloon against other materials like plastic, glass, or a balloon of the same material to compare the results.

Safety Guidelines

- Adult supervision is advised.

- Ensure the balloon is not overinflated to prevent any risks of bursting.

- Avoid rubbing the balloon against materials that may cause allergic reactions or release harmful particles.

Scientific Explanation

Static electricity is created when two objects with different electrical charges come into contact and then separate. When you rub the balloon against the fabric surface, electrons are transferred from the fabric to the balloon, leaving the balloon with a negative charge. The paper or light objects have a positive charge or neutral charge. Opposite charges attract, causing the paper or object to be attracted to the balloon due to the imbalance of charges. This experiment allows kids to observe the fun and interactive nature of static electricity and the principles of electrical charge attraction.

STEM Challenges

Now, let's move on to slightly complicated but fun experiments. STEM challenges are hands-on activities designed to engage children in the fields of science, technology, engineering, and mathematics (STEM). These challenges aim to promote critical thinking, problem-solving, creativity, and collaboration while applying scientific and mathematical concepts in practical, real-world contexts. Here are a few experiments you can attempt:

Building With Marshmallows and Toothpicks

Step-by-Step Instructions

1. Gather a variety of marshmallows and toothpicks for construction.

2. Encourage kids to use their creativity and imagination to build structures such as towers, bridges, or geometric shapes using the marshmallows as connectors and the toothpicks as support beams.

3. Experiment with different designs and configurations to see which structures are the strongest and most stable.

4. Test the structures by applying pressure or adding weight to see how they hold up.

Safety Guidelines

- Supervise young children to prevent ingestion of marshmallows or toothpicks.

- Be cautious of sharp ends of toothpicks to avoid accidental injuries.

- Avoid using marshmallows that may have been contaminated or have expired.

Scientific Explanation

This STEM challenge incorporates elements of engineering, physics, and geometry. The marshmallows act as connectors between the toothpicks, which serve as support beams in the structure. Children learn about the principles of stability, load-bearing capacity, and geometric shapes as they design and build their creations. By testing different structures, they can observe firsthand how the arrangement of materials impacts the strength and durability of the overall design.

Egg-Drop Challenge

Step-by-Step Instructions

1. Provide kids with a variety of materials such as newspapers, cardboard, bubble wrap, cotton balls, and tape.

2. Challenge them to design and construct a protective casing or device that will prevent a raw egg from breaking when dropped from a certain height.

3. Kids can test their designs by dropping the egg from increasing heights, starting from a low point and gradually increasing the elevation.

4. Evaluate and adjust the designs based on the outcomes of each test drop.

Safety Guidelines

- Use caution when handling raw eggs to prevent contamination.

- Choose an outdoor or safe indoor location for the egg drop to avoid accidents or mess.

- Avoid dropping the egg from extreme heights to prevent potential injuries.

Scientific Explanation

The egg-drop challenge engages kids in the principles of physics, engineering, and material science. By designing a protective casing for the egg, children learn about concepts such as structural integrity, shock absorption, and impact resistance. The challenge encourages them to think critically and creatively to come up with solutions that can minimize the forces acting on the egg during the drop. Through experimentation and iteration, they can understand how different materials and designs influence the outcome of the challenge.

Paper Airplane Contest

Step-by-Step Instructions

1. Provide kids with sheets of paper and encourage them to fold and create their own paper airplane designs.

2. Experiment with different folding techniques, wing shapes, and sizes to see how they affect the flight of the paper airplanes.

3. Host a contest where kids can test their paper airplanes for distance, accuracy, or aerobatics.

4. Allow kids to modify and refine their designs between rounds to improve performance.

Safety Guidelines

- Ensure that paper airplanes are flown in a safe area away from obstacles or people.

- Supervise children to prevent any potential accidents or collisions during the contest.

- Remind participants to be mindful of others' safety when launching their paper airplanes.

Scientific Explanation

The paper airplane contest is a hands-on activity that introduces kids to the principles of aerodynamics, flight dynamics, and engineering. By experimenting with different designs and flight characteristics, children can observe how factors such as wing shape, weight distribution, and air resistance influence the performance of their paper airplanes. As they iterate on their designs and test them in a controlled environment, they gain insight into the scientific principles that govern the behavior of flying objects.

Nature Science

Nature science involves observing, experimenting, and understanding the various phenomena that occur in nature. Below are a few fun experiments.

Plant-Growing Experiments

Step-by-Step Instructions

1. Ask the kids to choose the types of plants they want to grow for their experiment. Consider variables such as sun exposure, water requirements, and growth time.

2. Prepare the soil or growing medium for the plants. You can use small pots or trays for this experiment.

3. Plant the seeds according to the instructions provided for each plant type.

4. Place the plants in different environments to test variables such as sunlight, water, or soil types.

5. Regularly measure and record the growth of the plants, noting any differences between the different conditions.

6. Analyze and interpret the results to draw conclusions about the impact of various conditions on plant growth.

Safety Guidelines

- Handle seeds and growing materials carefully to avoid any ingestion or skin irritation.

- Choose nontoxic plants for the experiment to protect children.

Scientific Explanation

- Plant-growth experiments help demonstrate how environmental factors such as light, water, and soil nutrients affect plant growth.

- The experiment can also provide insights into the principles of photosynthesis and plant physiology.

Weather Station Creation

Step-by-Step Instructions

1. Gather the necessary equipment, such as a thermometer, a barometer, an anemometer, and a rain gauge.

2. Choose a suitable location to set up the weather station, ensuring it is away from obstructions and reflective surfaces that could affect readings.

3. Install each instrument according to its specific instructions, ensuring they are level and secure.

4. Regularly record readings from each instrument, including temperature, barometric pressure, wind speed, and rainfall.

5. Use the recorded data to analyze and predict weather patterns.

Safety Guidelines

- Ensure proper installation of equipment to prevent damage or accidents.

- Ask children to use appropriate safety measures when installing instruments up high or in exposed locations.

Scientific Principles

- Weather station creation demonstrates the collection and interpretation of weather data, which is essential for understanding and predicting weather patterns and climate changes.

- Understanding the principles of each weather instrument helps explain factors such as air pressure, temperature, and wind speed.

Bug Habitat Observation

Step-by-Step Instructions

1. Create a habitat for bugs using a terrarium or a DIY enclosure with suitable materials such as soil, plants, and hiding spots.

2. Observe and record the behavior and interactions of the bugs within the habitat.

3. Ask children to note any changes in behavior or habitat utilization over time.

4. Research the species of bugs in the habitat to better understand their behavior and environmental needs.

5. Analyze the observations to draw conclusions about bug behavior and habitats.

Safety Guidelines

- Handle bugs gently and avoid disturbing their natural behavior unnecessarily.

- Research any potential risks associated with the specific bug species and take appropriate precautions, so children stay safe.

Scientific Principles

- Bug habitat observation allows for the study of ecosystems, predator–prey relationships, and the adaptation of species to their environment.

- Understanding bug behavior and habitats contributes to ecological awareness and biodiversity conservation efforts.

Fun With Chemistry

Chemistry involves understanding the composition, structure, properties, and changes of matter. Fun with chemistry allows for hands-on exploration of the principles of chemistry through the following activities:

Making Slime

Step-by-Step Instructions

1. Mix together glue, food coloring, and any additional glitter or decorations in a plastic container.

2. Add liquid starch to the mixture in small amounts, stirring well after each addition.

3. Continue adding starch until the mixture forms a slime consistency.

4. Knead the mixture, stretching and shaping the slime to enhance its texture and elasticity.

5. Store the slime in an airtight container.

Safety Guidelines

- Make slime in a well-ventilated area to avoid inhaling fumes.

- Avoid contact with the eyes and mouth; wash your hands after making the slime.

- Ensure that children do not ingest the slime or any ingredients.

Scientific Principles

- Making slime involves the principles of polymers and cross-linking, which creates the stretchy, elastic texture of the slime.

- Liquid starch serves as a cross-linker that binds the polymer molecules in the glue, creating a network of interconnected molecules that form the slime.

Homemade Playdough

Step-by-Step Instructions

1. Combine flour, salt, cream of tartar, and vegetable oil in a mixing bowl.

2. In a separate saucepan, mix water and food coloring until dissolved.

3. Add the dry ingredients to the saucepan and heat over medium heat, stirring continuously.

4. Continue to cook the mixture until it forms a dough consistency.

5. Remove the dough onto a clean working surface and knead until it becomes soft and pliable.

6. Store the playdough in an airtight container.

Safety Guidelines

- Keep food coloring off hands, mouth, and clothes of children.

- Store the playdough in an airtight container when not in use.

Scientific Principles

- The homemade playdough recipe involves the principles of non-Newtonian fluids and the stabilization of particles.

- The cream of tartar helps stabilize the salt crystals, which help the playdough keep its texture.

Baking Soda and Vinegar Reactions

Step-by-Step Instructions

1. Place baking soda in a mixing bowl.

2. Pour vinegar into a separate bowl.

3. Add vinegar to the baking soda and watch the chemical reaction.

4. Observe carbon dioxide bubbles form as a result of the reaction.

Safety Guidelines

- Protect children from any splashes by using a deep bowl for the experiment.

- Maintain a safe distance from the reaction.

Scientific Principles

- A chemical reaction occurs because baking soda, a base, reacts with vinegar, an acid, resulting in the release of carbon dioxide gas.

- The reaction follows the principle of the law of conservation of mass, which states that mass cannot be created or destroyed in a chemical reaction.

Engaging children in these hands-on science experiments not only sparks their curiosity and creativity but also helps them develop a deeper understanding of the natural world and scientific principles. Encouraging children to observe, question, and experiment with the world around them lays the foundation for a lifelong appreciation of science and discovery. As we wrap up this chapter on science experiments and exploration for children, let's head to Chapter 5 and explore the exciting world of cooking and baking, where children can further explore the wonders of creativity in the kitchen.

Chapter 5:

Cooking and Baking

Cooking with kids is not just about ingredients, recipes, and cooking. It's about harnessing imagination, empowerment, and creativity. –Guy Fieri

Summer offers a treasure trove of delicious and enticing delights, from sizzling barbecues to refreshing frozen treats. It's a time when families come together to share a meal, create lasting memories, and delight in the rich flavors of the season. However, what if we told you that the joy of summer dining can extend beyond the sizzling grill and the cheerful gatherings? What if we shared a secret recipe for infusing even more delight into this season of culinary decadence? In this chapter, we invite you to embark on a remarkable journey that revolves around cooking and baking with kids, transforming them into the chefs of their summer culinary adventures.

By engaging kids in the art of preparing food, we not only help them develop their creativity and curiosity but also lay the foundation for a lifelong love of cooking. From whipping up whimsical treats to flipping hearty pancakes, this chapter will unravel a world of culinary exploration that kids can embark upon during the sun-soaked months of summer (Fortin, 2021).

Additionally, through cooking and baking, children learn the significance of teamwork, accountability, and cooperation. Whether it's setting the table for a shared family meal or collaborating on a grand culinary project, kids develop a sense of responsibility and teamwork that extends beyond the kitchen into their daily lives. This chapter explores how culinary activities can nurture these essential values amid the aromas and textures of delicious concoctions.

Safety Precautions for Cooking With Kids

Cooking with kids can be a great bonding experience and an opportunity to teach them essential life skills. However, it is important to prioritize safety in the kitchen to prevent accidents and ensure a positive experience for all involved. Here are some key safety precautions to keep in mind when cooking with kids:

- **Supervision:** Adult supervision is crucial when cooking with children, especially when handling hot ingredients or using kitchen appliances. Supervision ensures that children are not exposed to harmful situations, and allowances are well taken in case they encounter difficulties.

- **Food allergies:** Before preparing any recipe, always ask the children and their families if they have any food allergies. Use substitutions for ingredients that might cause allergic reactions.

- **Choking hazards:** Young children are at a greater risk of choking on small ingredients. Use age-appropriate ingredients like larger chocolate chips instead of mini–chocolate chips, which will reduce the choking hazard. Also, make sure they are seated and that age-appropriate utensils are used.

- **Hot surfaces:** The oven, stove, and other cooking equipment can reach very high temperatures, so it is essential to teach children to be cautious while using them. Keep oven mitts within reach and instruct children to use them when handling hot trays or pans. Also, teach them not to touch or go near hot surfaces.

- **Sharp utensils:** Knives, forks, and other sharp utensils should be handled with care, especially when using them with children. Show children how to hold and use the knives properly. Ensure the knives are sharp to avoid slippage, and encourage them to use a cutting board when cutting fruit and vegetables.

- **Washing and prepping fruit:** Thoroughly wash and prepare fruit before cutting them to reduce the risk of food-borne illnesses. Teach children the proper way of washing and storing fresh produce, and what to look for when identifying fruit that may be spoiled.

Easy Recipes for Kids

Introduce your little ones to the joy of cooking with these simple, fun recipes that are perfect for children who want to get involved in the kitchen. These recipes are sure to spark their interest in culinary creations (Fortin, 2021).

No-Bake Treats

Ingredients

- 2 cups rolled oats

- 1/2 cup peanut butter

- 1/3 cup honey

- 1/2 cup mini–chocolate chips

- 1 teaspoon vanilla extract

Instructions

1. In a large bowl, mix together the rolled oats, peanut butter, honey, chocolate chips, and vanilla extract.

2. Stir until well combined and the mixture sticks together.

3. Roll the mixture into small balls and place them on a baking sheet lined with parchment paper.

4. Refrigerate the balls until firm—around 30 minutes.

5. Enjoy these delicious no-bake treats as a quick and easy snack!

Simple Cookie Recipes

Ingredients

- 1 cup all-purpose flour

- 1/2 cup unsalted butter, softened

- 1/3 cup granulated sugar

- 1 teaspoon vanilla extract

- A pinch of salt

Instructions

1. Preheat the oven to 350 °F (180 °C) and line a baking sheet with parchment paper.

2. In a mixing bowl, cream together the butter and sugar until light and fluffy.

3. Add the vanilla extract and beat until combined.

4. Gradually mix in the flour and salt until a dough forms.

5. Roll the dough into small balls and place them on the baking sheet.

6. Flatten each ball with a fork to create a crisscross pattern.

7. Bake the cookies for 10–12 minutes or until golden brown.

8. Let the cookies cool on a wire rack before serving.

Fruit Skewers

Ingredients

- Assorted fruit (such as strawberries, grapes, pineapple, and melon)
- Wooden skewers

Instructions

1. Wash and prepare the fruit by cutting them into bite-sized pieces.

2. Thread the fruit pieces onto the wooden skewers in any pattern you like.

3. Refrigerate the fruit skewers for a refreshing and healthy treat on a hot summer day.

4. Get creative with different fruit combinations and enjoy these colorful and tasty skewers!

Fun With Food

Here are some fun recipes that kids will love trying. They may love eating these, but do they know how to make them? Let's give it a try.

DIY Pizza

Ingredients

- Pizza dough (store-bought or homemade)
- Pizza sauce

- Cheese (e.g., mozzarella, cheddar, or any preferred cheese)

- Toppings of choice (e.g., sliced vegetables, pepperoni, cooked chicken)

Instructions

1. Preheat the oven to the temperature specified on the pizza dough package or recipe.

2. Roll out the pizza dough on a lightly floured surface to your desired thickness.

3. Transfer the dough to a pizza stone or baking sheet lined with parchment paper.

4. Spread a thin layer of pizza sauce over the dough, leaving a small border around the edges.

5. Sprinkle a generous amount of cheese evenly over the sauce.

6. Add your preferred toppings on top of the cheese.

7. Bake the pizza in the preheated oven for the time specified on the pizza dough package or recipe until the crust is golden and the cheese is melted and bubbly.

8. Allow the pizza to cool slightly before cutting into slices and enjoying!

Homemade Vanilla Ice Cream

Ingredients

- 2 cups heavy cream

- 1 cup whole milk

- 3/4 cup granulated sugar

- 2 teaspoons vanilla extract

- Ice

- Rock salt

Instructions

1. In a mixing bowl, combine the heavy cream, whole milk, granulated sugar, and vanilla extract. Stir until the sugar is dissolved.

2. Pour the mixture into an ice cream maker.

3. Follow the manufacturer's instructions for your specific ice cream maker model to churn the ice cream.

4. While the ice cream is churning, prepare an ice-salt mixture in a larger container or bucket. Layer ice and rock salt in the container.

5. Once the ice cream has thickened and reached the desired consistency (about 20–30 minutes), remove it from the ice cream machine and transfer it to a freezer-safe container.

6. Place the ice cream container in the ice–salt mixture, making sure the mixture surrounds the container.

7. Cover the container with a lid or plastic wrap and let it sit in the ice-salt mixture in the freezer for at least 2 hours or until the ice cream is firm.

8. Once the ice cream is firm, it is ready to be enjoyed!

Creative Sandwich-Making

Ingredients

- Bread (white, whole wheat, or preferred type)

- Assorted condiments and fillings (e.g., deli meats, cheese slices, lettuce, tomato, cucumber, mayo, mustard)

Instructions

1. Lay out two slices of bread on a clean surface.

2. Spread your preferred condiments (e.g., mayo, mustard) on one or both slices of bread.

3. Layer your desired fillings (e.g., deli meats, cheese, lettuce, tomato, and cucumber) on one of the bread slices.

4. Place the other bread slice on top to complete the sandwich.

5. Cut the sandwich into fun shapes using cookie cutters or simply cut it in half diagonally or horizontally.

6. Serve the creative sandwich and enjoy!

Berry-Picking to Make Jam

Ingredients

- Fresh berries (e.g., strawberries, blueberries, raspberries)

- Granulated sugar

- Pectin (optional)

Instructions

1. Start by going berry-picking and gather your desired amount of fresh berries.

2. Rinse the berries under cold water and remove any stems or leaves.

3. In a large pot, combine the berries and an equal amount of granulated sugar. If using pectin, follow the package instructions for the recommended amount.

4. Mash the berries using a potato masher or fork to release their juices.

5. Place the pot over medium heat and bring the mixture to a boil, stirring constantly.

6. Continue boiling and stirring for the time specified on the pectin package or until the mixture thickens and reaches the desired jam consistency.

7. Remove the pot from the heat and let the jam cool for a few minutes.

8. Transfer the jam to clean, sterilized jars and seal them tightly.

9. Allow the jars to cool completely before refrigerating or storing them in a cool, dark place.

10. Enjoy the homemade jam on toast, pancakes, or any other preferred way!

Healthy Snacks

Who doesn't love healthy eating? However, the problem is healthy food isn't always readily available. Why not teach kids how to make them?

Veggie Art

Ingredients

- Assorted vegetables (e.g., bell peppers, cucumbers, cherry tomatoes, carrots, celery)

- Hummus or your favorite dip

- Cheese slices

- Pretzels or crackers

- Olives

- Optional: small, edible decorations like edible googly eyes, seeds, or nuts for decoration

Instructions

1. Wash and prepare the assorted vegetables by cutting them into various shapes and sizes.

2. Arrange the vegetables on a plate to create fun and colorful designs or patterns.

3. Use cheese slices, pretzels, or crackers to add extra details and textures to your veggie art.

4. Serve the veggie art with hummus or your favorite dip for dipping.

5. Get creative and have fun with your veggie-art designs before enjoying the colorful and nutritious snack!

Smoothie Creations

Ingredients

- Assorted fruit (e.g., bananas, berries, mango, pineapple)

- Spinach or kale (optional for added nutrition)

- Yogurt (plain or flavored)

- Milk or dairy-free alternative (e.g., almond milk, coconut milk)

- Honey or maple syrup (optional for added sweetness)

- Ice cubes

Instructions

1. Add the assorted fruit, spinach or kale, yogurt, milk, and honey or maple syrup (if desired) to a blender.

2. Blend the ingredients until smooth and well combined.

3. Add ice cubes to the blender and blend again until the smoothie reaches your preferred consistency.

4. Taste the smoothie and adjust the sweetness or thickness as needed by adding more honey, milk, or ice.

5. Pour the smoothie into glasses and garnish with fresh fruit slices or mint leaves, if desired.

6. Enjoy your custom smoothie creation filled with delicious fruit and nutrients!

Trail Mix Assembly

Ingredients

- Nuts (e.g., almonds, peanuts, cashews, walnuts)

- Dried fruit (e.g., raisins, cranberries, apricots, banana chips)

- Seeds (e.g., sunflower seeds, pumpkin seeds, chia seeds)

- Dark chocolate chips or chunks

- Pretzels or popcorn

- Optional: coconut flakes, mini-marshmallows, cinnamon

Instructions

1. In a large mixing bowl, combine the nuts, dried fruit, seeds, dark chocolate, and other desired ingredients.

2. Toss the ingredients together until well mixed.

3. Portion the trail mix into individual serving sizes or store it in an airtight container for later snacking.

4. Get creative with your own trail mix combinations by adjusting the quantities of each ingredient to suit your taste preferences.

5. Enjoy the trail mix as a convenient and nutritious snack any time!

Baking Challenges

Baking with kids can be a wonderful way to spend time together and unleash creativity in the kitchen. These baking challenges offer opportunities for kids to explore decorating, themed treats, and even basic baking skills like bread-making in a fun and interactive way.

Cupcake Decorating

Ingredients

- Premade cupcakes (homemade or store-bought)
- Buttercream frosting (homemade or store-bought)
- Assorted food coloring (gel or liquid)
- Sprinkles, edible glitter, chocolate shavings, or other decorations
- Piping bags and assorted piping tips
- Optional: fondant, edible flowers, small candies

Instructions

1. Prepare the buttercream frosting and divide it into separate bowls, if using different colors.

2. Add a small amount of the chosen food coloring to each portion of frosting and mix until the desired color is achieved.

3. Fit each piping bag with a different piping tip and fill each with the colored frosting.

4. Let the kids unleash their creativity by decorating the cupcakes with the colorful frosting, sprinkles, and other decorations.

5. Encourage them to experiment with different piping techniques and create their own unique designs on the cupcakes.

6. Once the cupcakes are decorated, let the kids enjoy their beautiful creations as a delicious treat!

Themed Cake Pops

Ingredients

- Cake mix and required ingredients for baking the cake

- Frosting (store-bought or homemade)

- Lollipop sticks

- Candy melts or chocolate chips

- Assorted sprinkles, edible glitter, or themed decorations

- Optional: edible markers, small candies, food coloring

Instructions

1. Bake the cake according to the package or recipe instructions and let it cool completely.

2. Crumble the cake into fine crumbs in a large mixing bowl.

3. Add a dollop of frosting to the cake crumbs and mix until the mixture is moist enough to hold its shape when rolled into balls.

4. Form the cake and frosting mixture into small balls and insert a lollipop stick into each ball.

5. Melt the candy melts or chocolate chips according to the package instructions.

6. Dip each cake pop into the melted-candy coating, allowing any excess to drip off, and then immediately decorate with sprinkles or other themed decorations.

7. Let the kids get creative by drawing fun faces or designs on the cake pops using edible markers.

8. Allow the cake pops to set before enjoying these delightful and themed sweet treats!

Bread-Baking Basics

Ingredients

- 4 cups all-purpose flour

- 2 1/4 teaspoons active dry yeast

- 1 1/2 teaspoons salt

- 1 1/2 cups warm water

- 2 tablespoons granulated sugar

- Optional: egg wash (1 egg whisked with 1 tablespoon water), sesame seeds, poppy seeds

Instructions

1. In a large mixing bowl, combine the warm water, sugar, and active dry yeast. Let it sit until it becomes foamy—about 5–10 minutes.

2. Add the flour and salt to the yeast mixture and mix until it forms a shaggy dough.

3. Turn the dough out onto a lightly floured surface and knead it until it becomes smooth and elastic—about 10 minutes.

4. Place the dough in a greased bowl, cover it with a kitchen towel, and let it rise in a warm place until it doubles in size—about 1–1.5 hours.

5. Preheat the oven to 400 °F (200 °C).

6. Punch the dough down and shape it into a loaf or rolls.

7.   Place the shaped dough on a baking sheet lined with parchment paper. If making a loaf, you can slash the top with a sharp knife.

8.   If desired, brush the surface of the dough with an egg wash—it helps bread get that golden-brown shine on top—and sprinkle with sesame seeds or poppy seeds.

9.   Bake the bread in the preheated oven for about 25–30 minutes for rolls or 30–35 minutes for a loaf, until golden brown and hollow-sounding when tapped on the bottom.

10. Let the baked bread cool before slicing and enjoying the homemade, freshly baked bread!

Create a Cookbook

Encouraging kids to create their own cookbook or recipe binder is a wonderful idea to foster their creativity, organization skills, and passion for cooking and baking. Here's a simple guide to help kids get started on their very own cookbook:

1.   **Choose recipes:** Have the kids select their favorite recipes that they have enjoyed making and eating. This could include the healthy snacks, baking challenges, and any other dishes they have prepared.

2.   **Gather materials:** Provide the kids with a binder or a notebook, transparent sheet protectors, lined paper, or premade recipe cards. They can also use colorful pens, markers, and stickers to make their cookbook visually appealing.

3.   **Take photos:** Encourage the kids to take photos of the dishes they have made. These photos can be printed and added to the cookbook along with the recipes. You can also create fun captions or stories to accompany the photos.

4. **Recipe writing and organizing:** Have the kids write down the ingredients and step-by-step instructions for each recipe in their own words. They can also include any tips or modifications they have discovered. Organize the recipes by categories such as snacks, desserts, main dishes, or whatever they desire.

5. **Visual creativity:** Let the kids use their creativity to decorate the recipe pages with drawings, doodles, and stickers. They can also use cut-outs from food magazines or create their own illustrations to accompany the recipes.

6. **Making it personal:** Encourage them to add a personal touch by including stories, memories, or reasons why they love each recipe. This can make the cookbook feel more like a cherished keepsake.

7. **Final touches:** Once all the recipes, photos, and personal touches are added, help the kids arrange the pages neatly in the binder or notebook. They can also decorate the cover and spine to make it truly their own.

By creating a cookbook, kids not only document their favorite recipes but also develop an appreciation for cooking, enhance their writing and organizational skills, and create a lasting keepsake filled with memories of time spent in the kitchen.

As you enjoy the aroma of freshly baked cookies and pies that fill the kitchen, and the laughter of children echoes through the house, you'll realize that cooking and baking bring an abundance of joy and memories.

As the summer days continue, children will look for new ways to keep themselves entertained and make each day special. Themed days and events are quickly becoming a favorite pastime, offering a chance to immerse children in creativity and imagination. From pirate treasure hunts to superhero costume parties, they will embrace the opportunity to explore different themes and bring their ideas to life. Chapter 6 does just that.

Chapter 6:

Themed Days and Events

Life is a circus ring, with some moments more spectacular than others.
–Janusz Korezak

As we've seen throughout this book, summer is a time of boundless opportunities for adventure, exploration, and joyful moments under the sun (and inside, too). In this chapter, we explore the enchanting realm of themed days and events. From superhero costume extravaganzas to exploring world crafts, the imagination knows no bounds when it comes to crafting unique and engaging experiences for children.

What sets this chapter apart is its emphasis on the dual nature of themed events and days—they can be both community-based and homegrown. While summer is filled with special holidays and events in our communities, such as Fourth of July celebrations, local fairs, and outdoor concerts, the beauty of themed days and events lies in the fact that children can also create their own magical moments right in the comfort of their homes.

As we step into this chapter, let's open our minds to the infinite creativity that lies within each of us, let's embrace the spirit of playfulness and imagination, and let's create memories that will last a lifetime. Join your children on this enchanting journey (Liliana, 2021).

Theme Party Ideas

Themed parties are a fantastic way to inject a sense of excitement and adventure into hot summer days. They provide the perfect opportunity for kids to unleash their creativity, immerse themselves in imaginative play, and make lasting memories. Below are some captivating ideas that can be easily executed to create unforgettable experiences for children during the summer season:

Pirate Adventure Day

By immersing young adventurers in a thrilling journey filled with treasure hunts, hidden maps, and daring escapades, you can ignite their imaginations and create lasting memories. A pirate-themed party is the perfect setting for such an adventure, complete with costumes, eye patches, and bandanas to transform the young landlubbers into fearsome pirates ready to set sail.

Setting the Stage

To set the stage for an unforgettable pirate adventure, the first step is to deck out the party space with all the trappings of a high-seas expedition. Bring the spirit of the open ocean to life by decorating with props such as treasure chests overflowing with faux gold coins, weathered pirate flags fluttering in the breeze, and perhaps even a mock ship or mast. By creating a captivating environment, you can transport the young buccaneers into a world of adventure and intrigue from the moment they arrive.

Treasure Hunt Extravaganza

The centerpiece of the pirate adventure is, of course, the treasure hunt. To ensure an unforgettable experience, design a series of clues and riddles that will lead the young adventurers on an exhilarating search for hidden riches. Each clue should require them to use their wits and cunning to decipher the next step of the quest, building suspense and excitement as they draw closer to the ultimate treasure. Consider incorporating interactive elements like secret compartments and mysterious maps to enhance the sense of discovery and unraveling the mystery.

Crafting and Creativity

Incorporating DIY activities into the pirate-themed party can add a creative and personalized dimension to the festivities. Set up a crafting station where children can design and customize pirate hats and flags, allowing them to unleash their imaginations and create unique symbols of their pirate identity. This not only enhances the fun but also provides a tangible memento for them to cherish long after the adventure has ended.

Pirate Ship Play Area

Transforming a designated space, either indoors or outdoors, into a pirate ship play area is the crowning touch to the immersive experience. Utilize barrels and ropes to construct an imaginative ship deck, bustling with the energy and vitality of a genuine pirate vessel. Through this interactive play area, children can engage in role-playing, navigate the high seas, and embark on their very own epic voyage.

Safety Considerations

While creating an immersive pirate adventure is an exciting endeavor, you must always ensure the safety of all participants. Double-check that all props and equipment are child-friendly and free from potential hazards. Adult supervision is crucial, especially during activities like the treasure hunt and interactive play, to ensure that the young adventurers remain safe while fully immersing themselves in the whimsical world of piracy.

Superhero Training Camp

Letting children be powerful superheroes for a day of adventure and excitement involves several key components to create an immersive and unforgettable experience.

Superhero Costumes

To kick off the event, providing children with superhero capes, masks, and emblems can instantly transport them into the world of heroes. These costumes will not only help set the scene but also ignite their imaginations and get them ready for the day's heroic deeds.

Obstacle Course

The centerpiece of the training camp can be an obstacle course designed to test key superhero skills, such as agility, strength, and speed. This physical activity not only adds an element of challenge and fun but also helps children feel like they are truly training to be superheroes.

Superhero Training Stations

Setting up various stations for children to practice superhero skills like super strength, agility, and even crafting their own superhero identity can add an interactive and engaging element to the event. Children can rotate through these stations, honing their powers and developing their unique superhero personas.

Superhero-Themed Scavenger Hunt

A superhero-themed scavenger hunt can be a thrilling activity that engages young minds as they search for hidden clues and artifacts that lead them closer to a final goal. This scavenger hunt not only promotes teamwork and problem-solving but also adds an element of mystery and excitement to the day's activities.

"Save the City" Mission or Themed Craft Activity

To cap off the day, organizing a "save the city" mission, where children must work together to tackle a pretend crisis, or a themed craft activity, where they can create their own superhero accessories, can empower children to harness their creativity and imagination. This final activity allows children to put their newfound superhero skills to the test and feel like they have truly saved the day.

Safety Considerations

- **Supervision:** Ensure that there are enough adults present to supervise the children throughout the day. Each activity should have at least one adult to monitor and assist where necessary.

- **Obstacle course safety:** Make sure that the obstacle course is constructed with materials that are sturdy and safe for children. Inspect all equipment and obstacles before the event to ensure that they are safe to use and free from hazards.

- **Training stations safety:** Especially with stations that are designed to practice physical superhero skills, make sure that the equipment and activities are appropriate for the age range of the children. Provide clear instructions and demonstrate proper technique to reduce the risk of injury.

- **Scavenger hunt safety:** Before starting the scavenger hunt, remind children to stay within designated boundaries and not venture outside the designated area. Ensure that the scavenger hunt items are safe and appropriate for children to handle.

- **Sun and heat safety:** If the event is outdoors, make sure that there is plenty of shade, and provide plenty of water to keep the children hydrated. Sunscreen should be readily available and applied on the children as needed to prevent sunburn.

Beach Day at Home

Creating a beach day at home involves bringing elements of the seaside to the backyard in a fun and engaging way. Here is how to set up and execute a beach-themed day along with the necessary items and preparations needed:

Setting the Scene

- Transform a section of the backyard into a mini–beach area with inflatable pools or sandboxes to create the feeling of a coastal paradise. This will provide the perfect setting for a variety of beach-themed activities and games.

- Decorate the space with beach-themed decorations such as banners, flags, and other props to enhance the seaside atmosphere and make the backyard feel like a real beach getaway.

- Ensure that there is enough space for activities, whether indoor or outdoor, depending on the weather and available space. Tailoring the activities to the specific theme will help immerse children in the beach day experience.

Beach Day Activities

- Encourage children to don swimsuits, sunglasses, and sun hats to get into the beach spirit. Providing costumes and accessories matching the theme, such as pirate attire, superhero capes, or beachwear, can add an extra layer of fun and immersion.

- Organize beach-themed activities such as sandcastle-building competitions, beach-ball games, and seashell scavenger hunts to keep the children entertained and active throughout the day.

- Set up a mocktail or smoothie-making station where children can create their own tropical drinks, adding a taste of the tropics to the beach day experience.

- Include creative activities like decorating beach towels or designing seashell-and-bead jewelry to add a touch of creativity and personalization to the day's activities.

Culminating the Celebration

- End the beach day with a beach-themed picnic complete with beach snacks and refreshing treats like fruit skewers, sandwiches, popsicles, and cool beverages to keep the children refreshed and satisfied.

- Consider creating a beach-themed playlist with summery tunes to enhance the ambiance and bring the feeling of a beach party to the backyard.

- Encourage children to share their favorite moments of the day, and perhaps award small prizes or certificates for their participation in the various activities.

Items You'll Need

- Costumes and accessories matching the theme (e.g., pirate attire, superhero capes, beachwear)

- Decorations such as banners, flags, and themed props

- Supplies for themed activities (e.g., treasure-hunt clues, craft materials for superhero emblems, sandcastle tools)

- Food and beverages in line with the theme

- Space for activities, whether indoor or outdoor, tailored to the specific theme

Safety Considerations

When organizing a beach day at home for children, it's important to prioritize safety to ensure that the experience is enjoyable and risk-free. Here are some safety considerations to keep in mind:

- **Supervision:** Assign several responsible adults to supervise the children throughout the beach day, especially during water-related activities or games. Ensure that there is constant adult supervision to prevent accidents or emergencies.

- **Designated play area:** Establish clear boundaries for the beach area and ensure that children understand where they are (and are not) allowed to play. Keep an eye on younger children to prevent them from wandering into areas that may pose risks, such as deep water or rough terrain.

- **Water safety:** If incorporating water activities like inflatable pools or water play, make sure children are closely monitored at all times, even if the water level is shallow. Encourage the use of appropriate floatation devices for children who are not strong swimmers.

- **Sun protection:** Provide ample shade and sunscreen to protect children from the sun's harmful UV rays. Encourage children to wear hats, sunglasses, and lightweight clothing that covers their skin to prevent sunburn.

- **Hydration:** Keep children hydrated throughout the day by offering plenty of water and refreshing beverages. Avoid sugary drinks that can lead to dehydration and provide water-rich snacks like fruit to keep children hydrated.

- **First aid kit:** Have a fully stocked first aid kit on hand in case of minor injuries or accidents. Make sure that adults supervising the event are aware of the location of the first aid kit and know how to respond to common injuries.

Holiday Celebrations

Holidays are a time of joy, festivity, and community. By incorporating holiday celebrations into the summer season, children can experience the magic of these special occasions in unique and unexpected ways. Below are delightful ideas and essential components to execute holiday-themed celebrations designed to bring seasonal cheer during the summer.

Fourth of July Festivities

To bring the Fourth of July celebration to life for children, here are some suggestions and preparations for creating a fun and patriotic day:

Setting the Scene

- Set up a designated area in the backyard with decorations showcasing the colors of the American flag. Hang up American flags, patriotic buntings, and string lights to create a vibrant and festive atmosphere.

- Ensure that the space is safe with cleared paths and well-lit areas. Remove any potential hazards, such as sharp objects or slippery surfaces, to minimize the risk of accidents.

Fourth of July Activities

- Encourage children to dress in red, white, and blue attire to embrace the patriotic spirit. Provide party favors like temporary tattoos, bracelets, or hats for them to wear throughout the day.

- Organize classic Fourth of July games like potato sack races, three-legged races, and tug-of-war to keep children entertained and active. Divide them into teams and award small prizes or ribbons for their participation and achievements in the games.

- Set up a craft station where children can engage in creative activities such as making patriotic bracelets using red, white, and blue beads or designing flag-inspired artwork. Provide art supplies, templates, and ideas to inspire their creative expressions.

- Host a water-balloon toss or a water-balloon piñata activity to keep children cool and add some water fun to the celebration. Ensure proper supervision to maintain safety during water-related activities.

- Consider organizing a mini–fireworks show using child-friendly alternatives like glow sticks, confetti poppers, or sparklers. Teach children how to use these items safely and provide a designated open area for their use.

Culminating the Celebration

- As the evening progresses, gather children and families for a mini–fireworks display. Ensure that all fireworks or alternatives are handled safely and in compliance with local regulations. Prioritize safety by providing a clear, open space for fireworks and clear instructions for their use.

- Offer a variety of festive food and refreshing beverages to complement the celebration, such as themed cupcakes, fruit skewers, and lemonade. Ensure that all food is prepared, stored, and served following proper hygiene and safety guidelines.

- Create a playlist of patriotic songs to play throughout the day, igniting the feeling of national pride and enhancing the celebratory atmosphere.

Safety Considerations

- **Fireworks safety:** If using fireworks, follow local ordinances and regulations and use only child-friendly alternatives. Closely supervise children during their use, ensuring they are at a safe distance from others and handling them responsibly.

- **Sun protection:** Provide shade, sunscreen, and hats for children to protect them from the sun. Encourage frequent hydration and offer water-rich snack options.

- **Outdoor safety:** Remove any potential hazards from the designated area, such as sharp objects or slippery surfaces. Ensure proper lighting and clear pathways to prevent accidents or injuries.

Christmas in July

To bring the concept of Christmas in July to life, you can create a magical, festive experience for children during the summer season. Here's how you can bring this to life:

Decor

Transform the space into a winter wonderland by using faux snow, twinkling lights, and a Christmas tree decorated with a summer twist. Incorporate beach-themed ornaments, seashells, or tropical flowers to give the tree a unique and festive feel.

Activities

- **Gift exchange/Secret Santa:** Encourage children to participate in a gift exchange or Secret Santa activity to capture the joy of giving and receiving gifts. You can set a theme for the gifts, such as summer essentials or small personalized items.

- **Baking and cookie decorating:** Gather the children for a baking session where they can make Christmas-themed treats or decorate cookies with colorful icing and sprinkles. This hands-on activity will not only be fun but also gives them a chance to showcase their creativity.

- **Crafting ornaments and artwork:** Provide materials for the children to create their own ornaments or holiday-themed artwork. This DIY activity allows them to add a personal touch to the celebration and take home a memento of the event.

- **Winter-themed games:** Plan winter-themed games like a snowball toss using soft balls or a "melting snowman" race where children stack and dismantle snowman decorations. These games will bring laughter and excitement to the event.

Safety Considerations

When organizing this celebration for children, it's important to prioritize safety considerations. Here are a few tips to ensure a safe and fun event:

- **Decorations:** Ensure that all the decorations used are flame-retardant or flame-resistant. Do not use lighted candles or any open flames around children.

- **Baking and food handling:** Making baked goods should be supervised by an adult. Make sure children understand the importance of washing hands and using clean utensils while preparing food. Also, inform children of any dietary restrictions or allergens before engaging in any baking activities.

- **Crafting materials:** When providing crafting materials, make sure that they are nontoxic and safe for children. Avoid sharp objects or materials that can break easily and cause injury.

- **Games:** Before conducting any games, make sure children understand the rules and guidelines for safe play. Set up boundaries and ensure that the area where games will take place is free of any obstacles.

- **Supervision:** Assign a few adults or caregivers to supervise children to ensure their safety throughout the event.

Halloween in Summer

To bring the concept of Halloween in Summer to life, you can create a thrilling and fun-filled celebration with spooktacular delights. Here's what you can do:

- **Eerie decorations:** Transform the event space with spooky decorations such as cobwebs, faux spiders, and glowing jack-o'-lanterns to set a delightfully eerie and mysterious tone. You can use black-and-orange-themed props, flags, and lights to create a Halloween atmosphere.

- **Costume parade/contest:** Organize a costume parade where children can showcase their imaginative and festive attire. Consider offering prizes for various costume categories to encourage children to unleash their creativity.

- **Haunted house/spooky storytelling:** Set up a haunted house area or a space for spooky storytelling to add an element of thrilling adventure to the event. You can create themed areas with scary decorations and dim lighting to enhance the spooky atmosphere.

- **Halloween-themed crafts:** Provide children with the supplies to engage in Halloween-themed crafts such as decorating mini-pumpkins, creating ghostly artwork, or creating wearable witch hats. This will provide a bewitching artistic experience and allow children to tap into their creative side.

- **Themed treasure hunt/"mummy wrap" race:** Plan a themed treasure hunt where children can search for hidden Halloween-themed items or treats. Additionally, organize a "mummy wrap" race where children are divided into teams and race to wrap a team member in white bandages. These activities will infuse the celebration with spirited fun and excitement.

Safety Considerations

When organizing a Halloween in Summer celebration for children, it's important to prioritize safety considerations. Ensure that all the props, decorations, and materials used are child-friendly and safe. Avoid the use of any sharp or hazardous objects in crafting activities, and make sure that adult supervision is in place for all activities.

Cultural Days

Cultural days provide a wonderful opportunity for children to explore and embrace the world's diverse cultures. Through engaging activities and immersive experiences, children can celebrate the richness of global traditions, cuisine, art, and music. By creating a multicultural environment, they gain a deeper understanding and appreciation for the global community. Below are delightful ideas and essential components to execute cultural-themed days designed to bring out curiosity, understanding, and joy in children.

International Food Festivals

To create an engaging and educational international food festival for kids, you can offer a delectable journey through various cuisines and culinary traditions from around the world. Here's how to inspire children:

Global Food Market

- Set up a global food market with colorful, vibrant booths representing different countries and cultures. Each booth can showcase traditional clothing, artifacts, and information about the country's culinary heritage.

- Create an interactive passport activity, where children are given a passport to get stamped at each booth they visit, encouraging them to explore and learn about different cultures.

Sample Stations/Potluck-Style Event

- Offer sample stations with small portions of international dishes, allowing children to taste and experience flavors from around the world.

- Consider organizing a potluck-style event where participants, including children and their families, bring dishes from their cultural background to share and celebrate diversity.

Food-Related Activities

- **Cooking demonstration:** Host a cooking demonstration where a chef or adult volunteer prepares a simple kid-friendly international dish, explaining the cultural significance and ingredients.

- **Decorate-your-own-cupcake station:** Set up a station with plain cupcakes and an array of international toppings, such as tropical fruit, candies, or themed decorations, allowing children to create their own culinary masterpieces.

- **Culinary storytelling:** Arrange a storytelling session where children learn about the cultural and historical significance of various foods and dishes from different parts of the world, accompanied by engaging visuals or props.

Educational Materials

- Provide information sheets or small booklets with fun facts about different cuisines and culinary traditions from around the world.

- Create a map or display showcasing the countries represented in the festival, along with interesting facts about their food culture and traditional dishes.

Cultural Performances

- Integrate cultural performances such as traditional dances or music from various countries to add an entertaining and immersive element to the festival.

Around-the-World Crafts

Introducing children to the arts and crafts of different cultures can be an excellent way to encourage creativity and teach them appreciation for diverse artistic traditions. Here's a plan for creating a multicultural arts-and-crafts event for children:

Craft Stations

- Set up individual craft stations, each featuring crafts from different countries or cultures. For example, you can feature Japanese origami, African mask-making, Mexican papel picado, Indian Rangoli, Native American dreamcatchers, and more. Each station should be colorfully decorated to represent the culture it features.

Craft Activities

- Provide children with the necessary materials and instructions for creating traditional crafts from each culture. For example, at the Japanese origami station, kids can learn to fold paper into cranes or other origami shapes. At the African mask-making station, they can use colorful papers, feathers, and other art supplies to create masks. At the Mexican papel picado station, kids can learn to cut intricate designs into colorful tissue paper.

Storytelling and Cultural Significance

- Incorporate storytelling sessions at each station to share the cultural significance and history behind the craft. This will not only engage children in the craft-making process but also provide them with valuable insight into the traditions and stories associated with each art form.

Craft Passports and "Travel" Experiences

- Encourage children to craft their own passports at the beginning of the event. These passports can have designated spaces for stamps or stickers from each station they visit.

- As children complete a craft at each station, they can receive a stamp or sticker in their passport, simulating a journey through different cultures. This will create a playful and immersive experience, allowing children to "travel" and explore different artistic traditions.

Educational Materials and Displays

- Provide educational materials such as posters, books, or information sheets displaying the art and crafts of each culture. These materials can include fun facts, pictures, and brief descriptions of the significance of each craft.

Hands-on Experience

- Offer a hands-on experience by having adult volunteers or experts at each station to guide and assist children in creating their crafts. This will ensure that children receive proper guidance and support while exploring different artistic traditions.

Music and Dance From Different Cultures

Exploring the rich variety of rhythms, melodies, and movements from diverse cultures through music and dance can offer children an enriching learning experience. Here's how to incorporate music and dance into a multicultural event for kids:

Demonstrations and Performances

- Arrange live demonstrations or performances showcasing traditional dances from various cultures. For example, you can feature Indian Bollywood dance, Irish step dance, African tribal dances, Native American powwow dances, and more. Consider inviting local cultural dance groups or instructors to perform and engage children with dynamic and captivating displays of global diversity.

Hands-on Music Experiences

- Set up interactive stations with instruments from around the world, such as drums, tambourines, maracas, and more. Provide children with the opportunity to experiment with different sounds, rhythms, and beats, allowing them to engage in a tactile exploration of various musical traditions.

- Include knowledgeable volunteers or musicians at each station to guide children and share information about the cultural significance of the instruments and their unique sounds.

Multicultural Dance Party

- Organize a multicultural dance party or workshop where children can groove to a diverse playlist of international music. Feature a mix of traditional and contemporary tunes from different countries to create a festive and celebratory atmosphere.

- Consider incorporating dance tutorials or interactive sessions led by instructors to teach children simple steps or moves from different cultural dances, encouraging them to participate and learn new dance styles.

Cultural Context and Significance

- Before each performance or dance session, provide brief introductions or storytelling about the cultural context and significance of the dance forms being showcased. This will deepen children's understanding and appreciation for the rich history and traditions behind the movements and rhythms.

Costumes and Props

- Enhance the visual experience by incorporating colorful costumes, props, and decorations that reflect the cultural aesthetics of the dances being featured. Consider setting up a photo booth with culturally themed props for children to take fun pictures and immerse themselves in the global dance experience.

Interactive Dance Activities

- Include interactive dance activities such as group dance circles, line dances, or partner dances that encourage children to participate and engage with the music and movements. This interactive element can create a sense of community and togetherness among participants.

DIY Carnivals and Fairs

Introducing children to carnivals and fairs can be a fun and engaging way to spark their creativity and imagination. From setting up game booths to preparing homemade carnival snacks and hosting talent shows, there are plenty of activities that can make for a memorable experience. Here are some ideas to consider:

Setting Up Game Booths

- Decide on a variety of carnival games, such as ring toss, bean bag toss, balloon darts, or duck pond.

- Prepare the necessary supplies for each game, such as rings, bean bags, balloons, and small prizes.

- Create colorful signage and decorations to make the game booths visually appealing.

- Assign volunteers or older children to run each game booth and explain the rules to younger participants.

Homemade Carnival Snacks

- Whip up classic carnival treats such as popcorn, cotton candy, caramel apples, snow cones, and homemade lemonade.

- Set up food stations with ingredients, equipment, and serving containers for each snack.

- Consider including healthier options such as fruit skewers, trail mix, or veggie cups for a balanced menu.

- Don't forget to provide napkins, cups, and utensils for easy snacking.

Talent Show and Performances

- Encourage children to showcase their talents through dance routines, singing performances, magic tricks, or skits.

- Set up a designated performance area with a stage or open space, as well as a sound system for music playback.

- Create a program schedule with a lineup of acts and allocate time slots for each performance.

- Encourage audience participation by providing cheering tools such as pom-poms, noisemakers, or glow sticks.

From superhero extravaganzas to international art, these special days will bring joy, creativity, and endless adventures. Buckle up and get ready to hit the road, as we embark on a new chapter filled with wanderlust and exploration. In Chapter 7, we'll uncover the secrets of making travel an unforgettable experience for kids. From roadside attractions to travel games, this chapter promises to ignite the spirit of adventure in children of all ages.

Chapter 7:

Let's Go! Road Trips and Travel

When you travel with children, you are giving something that can never be taken away: Experience, exposure, and a way of life. –Pamela Chandler

For many families, summer means packing up the car and heading out on a road trip. Whether you're traveling to a nearby state park or taking a cross-country adventure, road trips are a great way to see the world and spend quality time with your loved ones.

In this chapter, we'll explore the joys of traveling during the summer months with your kids, and how to make the most of your road trip experience (Nicolette, 2023). We'll share our top tips and tricks for planning a successful road trip, from in-car activities to planning camps.

Vacations and Planned Family Getaways

Summer is the perfect time for families to embark on vacations and planned getaways to create unforgettable memories together. Whether you're looking to relax on a beach or immerse yourself in nature, summer vacations provide a much-needed break from the routine of daily life and offer a chance to reconnect with your loved ones. Here are a few ideas:

Beach Vacations

Beach vacations are a classic choice for families looking to unwind and have fun in the sun. From building sandcastles to swimming in the ocean, beach destinations offer a variety of activities that cater to all ages. Kids can splash in the waves, collect seashells, or enjoy ice cream treats on the boardwalk. Parents can relax on the beach, soak up the sun, and take in the beautiful coastal views. Beach vacations provide a perfect blend of relaxation and excitement for the whole family.

Theme Park Adventures

For families seeking thrills and excitement, a trip to a theme park can be the ultimate summer getaway. Whether it's exploring the magical world of Disney or experiencing adrenaline-pumping rides at a thrill park, theme parks offer endless entertainment for kids and adults alike. From meeting favorite characters to indulging in delicious theme park treats, a theme park adventure is sure to create lasting memories for the entire family.

Outdoor Adventures

Nature lovers will appreciate a summer vacation centered around outdoor activities such as camping, hiking, or visiting national parks. Camping trips provide an opportunity to unplug from technology, bond with nature, and engage in fun activities like campfires, stargazing, and exploring nearby trails. Visiting national parks allows families to witness breathtaking landscapes, observe wildlife, and participate in ranger-led programs that educate and inspire. Outdoor adventures offer a chance for families to connect with the natural world and create lasting memories in the great outdoors.

City Explorations

If your family enjoys discovering new cultures, cuisines, and attractions, a city vacation could be the perfect choice. Cities offer a variety of family-friendly activities, such as visiting museums, exploring historic sites, and trying local cuisine. Kids can experience the hustle and bustle of city life, ride on public transportation, and immerse themselves in different cultures. City vacations provide a blend of education, entertainment, and exploration that will broaden children's horizons and create lasting impressions.

In-the-Car Activities and Games

Road trips are a quintessential part of summer, offering families the chance to experience memorable journeys and explore new destinations. However, long hours in the car can sometimes lead to restless children and boredom. To keep the kids entertained and engaged while on the road, here are some fun and creative in-the-car activities and games along with the materials needed and steps to play:

I-Spy

- **Materials needed:** None

- **How to play:** A classic game for road trips, I-Spy requires one person to choose an object within sight and say, "I spy something [color or description]." The other players then take turns guessing the object until someone guesses correctly. The person with the correct guess then begins the next round.

Travel Bingo

- **Materials needed:** Printable travel bingo cards (available online), markers, or stickers

- **How to play:** Distribute the bingo cards to each child and have them look out for items such as stop signs, license plates from different states, or specific landmarks. When they spot an item on their card, they mark it off. The first player to complete a row or column shouts "Bingo!"

Storytelling

- **Materials needed:** None

- **How to play:** Storytelling is a great way for kids to exercise their creativity. One person starts a story with a single sentence, and then each person in the car adds a sentence to continue the story. The story evolves with each addition, creating a collaborative and imaginative tale.

20 Questions

- **Materials needed:** None

- **How to play:** One player thinks of an animal, object, or famous person, and the other players take turns asking up to 20 yes-or-no questions to guess what the chosen item is. If a player correctly guesses the item before the 20 questions are up, they win the round and get to think of the next item.

License Plate Game

- **Materials needed:** Printed map of the United States

- **How to play:** Have each child mark off the license plates of different states they see on the map. The goal is to spot as many different state license plates as possible during the trip. This game can also spark conversations about geography and travel.

Car Karaoke

- **Materials needed:** Playlist of family-friendly songs, car stereo or portable speaker

- **How to play:** Select a variety of favorite songs and take turns being the lead singer. Encourage everyone to join in and sing along. This activity is a great way to lift spirits and create a fun, energetic atmosphere in the car.

By incorporating these in-the-car activities and games into your road trip, you can transform long hours on the road into enjoyable, memorable moments for the whole family. These games not only keep the kids entertained, but also encourage creativity, storytelling, and friendly competition, making the journey just as exciting as the destination.

Camping/Cabins—Lake Activities, Marshmallow Roasts, and Ghost/Campfire Stories

Summer camping or staying in cabins can be a fantastic way to create lasting memories and have fun with kids. Here's a detailed plan on how to go about doing this:

Materials Needed

- **Tent(s) or cabins:** Tents for camping or cabins at a suitable location—whichever you prefer

- **Camping gear:** Sleeping bags, air mattresses, camping chairs, lanterns, and mosquito repellent

- **Cooking supplies:** Camp stove, pots, pans, cooking utensils, dishes, and cutlery

- **Water activities:** Canoes, kayaks, paddle boards, or inflatable rafts

- **Outdoor games:** Frisbee, soccer ball, badminton set, or any other games your kids enjoy

- **Marshmallow roasting:** Skewers, marshmallows, graham crackers, and chocolate bars

- **Ghost/campfire stories:** Books containing spooky stories or access to online resources

How to Organize Everything

1. **Choose a suitable location:** Research camping grounds or cabin options near a lake or with access to water activities. Look for places with good amenities, such as bathrooms and showers, especially if this is your first camping experience.

2. **Make reservations:** Be sure to book your campsite or cabin ahead of time, especially during peak summer months, when the demand is high.

3. **Plan meals:** Prepare a menu for the duration of your trip. Keep it simple yet enjoyable for kids. Opt for easy-to-cook meals like hot dogs, hamburgers, or foil-packet meals. Don't forget to include snacks and drinks for the whole family.

4. **Set up camp:** If you're camping, start by setting up your tent(s) and organizing your camping gear. Make sure everyone has a comfortable sleeping arrangement. If you're staying in cabins, get familiar with the space and settle in.

5. **Lake activities:** Engage in various water activities such as swimming, canoeing, kayaking, or paddle boarding. Make sure you have the necessary safety gear, such as life jackets, and have someone supervise the kids while they're in the water.

6. **Beach fun:** If your campsite or cabin is located near a lake beach, organize beach games such as sandcastle building, volleyball, or beach treasure hunts.

7. **Marshmallow roasts:** Build a campfire in a designated fire pit or use a portable fire pit, if allowed. Provide marshmallows, graham crackers, and chocolate bars. Teach the kids how to

safely roast marshmallows and make s'mores. Enjoy the delicious treats together.

8. **Ghost/campfire stories:** As the night falls, gather around the campfire—or in the cabin—and indulge in some spooky ghost stories. You can get creative and invent your own stories or read from books or online resources. Make sure the stories are age appropriate.

9. **Outdoor games:** During the day, engage in outdoor games like frisbee, soccer, badminton, or any other activities your kids enjoy. This will keep them active and entertained.

10. **Nature exploration:** Take the opportunity to explore the surrounding nature by going for hikes, identifying plant species, or even birdwatching. Encourage your kids to engage with the natural environment and appreciate its beauty.

Remember to prioritize safety during your trip. Stay hydrated, protect yourselves from the sun, and follow any rules or guidelines provided by the camping site or cabin rental.

Fairs, Farmers' Markets, and Rodeos

1. **Finding events:** Begin by researching local fairs, farmers' markets, and rodeos happening in your area during the summer. Check online event listings, community boards, or social media for information on dates and locations.

2. **Planning ahead:** Once you've identified the events you want to attend, add them to your calendar and plan a schedule. Consider factors like travel time, parking, and any specific timings or activities you don't want to miss.

3. **Arriving early:** To make the most of your day, consider arriving early. This can help you beat the crowds, secure good

parking, and have more time to explore and enjoy everything the event has to offer.

4. **Packing essentials:** Prepare a bag with essentials such as sunscreen, hats, water bottles, snacks, wet wipes, hand sanitizer, and any necessary items for your kids. Comfortable shoes are a must, as these events often involve a lot of walking.

5. **Exploring the fair:** Once you arrive, start exploring the various attractions at the fair. Visit the carnival rides, games, petting zoos, and exhibits. Make a plan with your kids to ensure you don't miss out on anything they are especially excited about.

6. **Farmers' market fun:** Encourage your kids to sample local produce and snacks while at the farmers' market. Engage them in conversations with vendors to learn about the products being sold. Consider buying fresh fruit, vegetables, or homemade goods to take home.

7. **Rodeo entertainment:** If attending a rodeo, find a good spot to watch the action. Explain the different events to your kids, such as bull riding, barrel racing, or roping, and let them soak in the excitement of this unique experience.

8. **Food experience:** One of the highlights of these events is often the food. Treat your kids to fair favorites like cotton candy, corn dogs, funnel cakes, or freshly made lemonade. Encourage them to try new foods and flavors.

9. **Engaging in activities:** Many fairs offer hands-on activities for kids, such as crafts, face painting, or interactive exhibits. Participate in these to create fun memories and keep your kids entertained.

10. **Safety first:** Keep an eye on your kids at all times, especially in crowded areas. Establish a meeting point in case anyone gets separated. Follow any safety guidelines provided at the event to ensure a smooth and enjoyable experience for everyone.

11. **Capture the moments:** Don't forget to capture the special moments of the day. Take photos with your kids enjoying the various activities and displays. These memories will be cherished for years to come.

Museums and Libraries

Museums and libraries can offer enriching, educational experiences for kids. Start by researching local museums and libraries to identify those that cater to children. Look for special exhibits, interactive displays, story times, or hands-on activities offered during the summer.

Museums often have specific exhibits geared toward kids, such as natural history, science, art, or interactive displays. Choose exhibits that match your children's interests and provide an engaging learning experience. Check with your local library for summer reading programs, storytelling sessions, craft workshops, and other kid-friendly activities. Many libraries offer themed programs aimed at getting kids excited about reading and learning.

Before heading to the museum or library, pack a bag with essentials such as water bottles, snacks, a notebook, pencils, and any specific items needed for the visit. Consider bringing a camera to capture memorable moments. Once there, encourage your kids to take an active part in exploring the exhibits. Ask them questions, spark their curiosity, and engage in discussions about the things they find interesting.

Take full advantage of any hands-on activities, workshops, or demonstrations being offered. Engaging in these interactive experiences can enhance your children's understanding of the subject matter and make the visit more memorable. If visiting a library, participate in story time sessions, which can help develop a love of reading in your kids and introduce them to new books and stories.

Utilize the resources and materials available at the library to find new books to read together, explore educational games, or conduct research on topics of interest to your kids. Also, teach your kids about proper behavior in museums and libraries, emphasizing the importance of respecting the exhibits, using indoor voices, and following any rules or guidelines set by the venues.

Take the time to capture the moments you and your kids spend exploring the museum or library. Document their favorite exhibits, activities, or books they discovered to reminisce about later. After the visit, engage in a discussion with your kids about what they learned and enjoyed. Encourage them to share their thoughts and ask questions about anything that piqued their interest.

Day Camps

Summer day camps are an excellent option for keeping kids busy, engaged, and entertained during the summer months. These camps are typically organized by schools, community centers, or specialized organizations, and they offer a wide range of activities to cater to the diverse interests of children.

One of the key advantages of summer day camps is that they provide structure and routine for children. During the school year, kids are used to having a set schedule with classes, extracurricular activities, and homework. However, once summer begins, this routine is often disrupted, and children may feel a lack of structure. Day camps help fill this void by providing a daily schedule of activities, ensuring that children have a routine to follow.

Another significant benefit of summer day camps is that they promote socialization. Kids have the opportunity to interact with peers outside of their regular school environment and make new friends. This social aspect of day camps enhances their communication skills, builds teamwork abilities, and fosters new connections.

Day camps also encourage physical activity. Many camps offer a wide range of sports and outdoor activities such as swimming, hiking, soccer, basketball, and more. These activities not only keep children active and healthy but also help them develop coordination, agility, and physical fitness.

Moreover, summer day camps encourage independence in children. They provide an environment where kids can try new things, take on new challenges, and learn to be self-reliant. Whether it's learning a new sport, participating in arts-and-crafts projects, or solving problems during team-building activities, children have the opportunity to develop confidence in their abilities and become more independent.

One of the most exciting aspects of summer day camps is the chance for kids to explore and engage in activities they may not have had exposure to before. Camps often offer a wide range of options such as music, dance, drama, science, technology, and nature exploration. This exposure enables children to discover new interests and passions, nurturing their creativity and encouraging them to explore different areas of knowledge.

When selecting a summer day camp for your child, you should consider their interests, age, and the activities offered by the camp. There are specialized camps focusing on specific interests like sports, arts, or science, as well as general camps that offer a mix of activities. Additionally, parents should look for camps with qualified, experienced staff who prioritize safety and adhere to appropriate guidelines.

Family Reunions and Events

Family reunions and events during the summer can be a fantastic way to spend quality time with extended family and create memorable experiences for kids. Whether it's a simple backyard barbecue or a more elaborate gathering at a resort or vacation spot, these events offer numerous opportunities for summer fun and meaningful connections.

One of the key benefits of family reunions is the bonding and connection that takes place among family members. For children, it provides a chance to meet and interact with relatives they may not see often. Building relationships with cousins, aunts, uncles, and grandparents helps children cultivate a sense of belonging and deepens their understanding of their family heritage.

Family reunions often feature a wide range of fun and engaging activities suitable for kids of all ages. Games and sports such as relay races, sack races, treasure hunts, and water-balloon fights can get kids active and excited. Additionally, arts-and-crafts stations where children can unleash their creativity, face painting, and temporary tattoos, and even themed costume parties can add a playful touch to the gathering.

Educational opportunities are also present during family reunions. Older generations can share stories, anecdotes, and lessons from the past, passing down family values, traditions, and cultural heritage. This not only helps children gain a deeper understanding of their roots but also instills a sense of pride and identity.

Creating lifelong memories is a significant aspect of family reunions and events. Children have the chance to experience special moments together with their relatives, such as singing songs around a campfire, sharing meals, telling funny stories, or even participating in talent shows. These shared experiences become cherished memories that shape their relationships and create a strong bond among family members.

When planning a family reunion or event focused on kids, be sure to consider their age range and interests. Offering a mix of activities that cater to different age groups ensures that everyone can participate and enjoy themselves. Involving children in the planning process by asking for their input on games, activities, or themes can also help build their enthusiasm and engagement.

Setting up specific spaces for kids to play and interact is another way to make family reunions more enjoyable for children. Designating a kids' zone with age-appropriate toys, games, arts-and-crafts supplies, and even hiring a babysitter or providing adult supervision can create a safe and engaging environment for younger attendees.

As we continue our summer journey with kids, we bring to you a chapter that showcases the harmonious blend of technology and fun. In Chapter 8, we'll explore how technology can enhance our summer experiences, both at home and on the go. Through the lens of innovative gadgets, applications, and virtual experiences, we'll discover how technology can ignite the imagination, spark learning, and open doors to new adventures.

Join us as we unravel the excitement of interactive educational apps, virtual reality escapades, and the joyous tunes of kid-friendly podcasts. We'll share tips on how to create screen-time boundaries, encourage digital literacy, and ensure a balanced approach to technology usage during the summer months.

Chapter 8:

Tuned-In Technology

We don't have a choice on whether we use technology, the choice is how we use it.
—Unknown

Technology has become an integral part of our daily lives, for us and for many children. As the warmer months approach, parents and caregivers may find themselves wondering how to strike a balance between allowing their children to engage with technology and ensuring that they also have a fulfilling and enjoyable summer (*Managing Screen Time: Balancing Technology Use for Children*, 2024). This chapter aims to provide guidance and suggestions for incorporating technology into summer activities in a way that is constructive and enhances the overall experience for children (*Incorporating Technology into Children's Activities: Pros and Cons*, 2023).

Importance of Blending Technology With Various Activities

Incorporating technology into a child's summer activities can have a profound impact on their overall development and engagement in a variety of endeavors. By blending technology with multiple activities, parents can create a well-rounded, dynamic summer experience for their children.

Outdoor Activities

Utilizing technology in outdoor activities can enhance a child's exploration of the natural world and encourage them to engage with their surroundings in new and exciting ways. For example, nature-themed apps can provide guided information on local flora and fauna, turning a simple hike or nature walk into an educational adventure. GPS-enabled devices can be used for geocaching activities, where kids can follow coordinates to discover hidden treasures, creating a sense of curiosity and discovery.

By incorporating technology into outdoor activities, children can develop a deeper appreciation for nature and the environment, while also honing their problem-solving skills and spatial awareness. Technology can serve as a bridge between the physical and digital worlds, offering opportunities for hands-on learning and interactive engagement that can make outdoor experiences more stimulating and rewarding.

Indoor Activities

Indoor activities can be just as enriching when technology is thoughtfully integrated. Educational apps and games can provide children with opportunities to learn new skills, reinforce academic concepts, and engage in stimulating challenges. Virtual tours and online resources can transport children to new and exciting destinations, allowing them to explore the world from the comfort of their own home.

Technology can also be used to facilitate social interactions and collaborative projects, enabling children to connect with friends and family members virtually and engage in creative endeavors together. Whether it's coding a digital masterpiece, composing music with online tools, or participating in virtual book clubs or storytelling sessions, technology can open up a world of possibilities for indoor summer activities that are both fun and educational.

Creative Activities

Blending technology with creative activities offers children unique opportunities for self-expression, innovation, and artistic exploration. Digital tools and platforms can empower children to create multimedia projects, experiment with visual and sound editing, and share their creations with a global audience. Whether it's producing a podcast, designing a digital artwork, or crafting a stop-motion animation, technology can elevate traditional forms of creativity and inspire children to think outside the box.

Moreover, technology can serve as a catalyst for collaboration and community engagement, enabling children to connect with peers, mentors, and experts in various fields to cultivate their creative talents. Online workshops, virtual mentorship programs, and creative challenges can provide children with the guidance and inspiration they need to explore their interests, develop their skills, and share their creations with a wider audience.

Using Technology for Learning and Entertainment

Technology can play a large role in enhancing children's learning experiences and providing them with engaging forms of entertainment. By incorporating technology into educational and recreational activities, kids can reap a wide array of benefits that contribute to their cognitive development, creativity, and overall enjoyment. Here are some key advantages of using technology in these contexts:

- **Interactive learning:** Technology offers interactive and immersive learning experiences that can cater to different learning styles and preferences. Educational apps, games, and online resources can present information in a dynamic and engaging manner, encouraging kids to actively participate and explore concepts through hands-on activities and simulations.

- **Personalized learning:** Technology can adapt to individual learning needs and pace, providing personalized feedback and support to help children progress at their own rate. Adaptive learning platforms can tailor content to each child's strengths and challenges, ensuring that they receive targeted assistance and reinforcement in areas where they need it most.

- **Access to diverse content:** Through technology, kids have access to a wealth of educational materials, including ebooks, videos, virtual tours, and online courses. This exposure to diverse content can broaden their knowledge, spark their curiosity, and inspire them to explore new subjects and interests beyond the traditional classroom curriculum.

- **Developing critical skills:** Using technology for learning can help children develop essential skills such as problem-solving, critical thinking, digital literacy, and communication skills. Interactive games and puzzles can challenge their cognitive abilities, while creative tools can help them build their artistic expression and technological proficiency.

- **Engagement and motivation:** Technology has the power to make learning more engaging, entertaining, and motivating for kids. Gamification elements, rewards systems, and interactive features can capture their attention and sustain their interest in educational activities, turning learning into a fun and rewarding experience.

- **Fostering creativity:** Technology offers kids a platform for expressing their creativity and imagination through digital art, music composition, storytelling, animation, and other creative outlets. Digital tools and platforms enable children to experiment, innovate, and share their creations with others, promoting self-expression and innovation.

- **Enhancing entertainment options:** Technology provides a wide range of entertainment options for kids, from interactive games and apps to streaming services and virtual experiences. These digital entertainment platforms can offer age-appropriate content that sparks curiosity, promotes cultural awareness, and encourages social interaction with peers.

- **Parental involvement and monitoring:** Technology allows parents and caregivers to be actively involved in their children's digital activities, monitoring their screen time, setting limits, and guiding them toward educational and safe online content. Parental control features and monitoring tools enable adults to support and guide their children's technology use in a responsible and positive manner.

Ensuring Safe, Mindful, and Balanced Tech Usage

Children's access to technology brings with it the importance of ensuring their online safety and privacy, as well as promoting mindful and balanced tech usage. By implementing strategies and guidelines, parents can help children navigate the digital landscape responsibly and securely. Here are some tips to ensure safe and balanced tech usage for kids:

- **Establish clear guidelines.** Set clear rules and expectations for tech usage, including screen-time limits, appropriate websites and apps, and guidelines for online communication. Establishing boundaries from an early age can help children develop healthy tech habits and understand the importance of balance in their digital interactions.

- **Educate kids about online safety.** Teach children about the importance of online safety, including the risks of sharing personal information online, interacting with strangers, and engaging in potentially harmful activities. Encourage open communication and provide resources on how to stay safe online, such as recognizing phishing scams, protecting passwords, and reporting inappropriate content.

- **Use parental controls.** Utilize parental control features on devices and apps to monitor and manage your child's online activities. These tools can help restrict access to certain websites, set time limits for screen time, and track your child's digital interactions to ensure they are engaging in safe and appropriate content.

- **Model healthy tech habits.** Children learn by example, so it's important for parents to model healthy tech habits and demonstrate balanced tech usage. Show children how to use technology mindfully, set boundaries for your own screen time, and prioritize face-to-face interactions and offline activities.

- **Encourage privacy settings.** Teach children how to adjust privacy settings on social media platforms, gaming consoles, and other online services to control who can see their information and activities. Emphasize the importance of safeguarding personal data and the risks of oversharing online.

- **Discuss their digital footprint.** Help children understand the concept of a digital footprint and how their online actions can have lasting consequences. Encourage them to think before posting, be mindful of their online presence, and consider how their digital activities could impact their reputation and future opportunities.

- **Promote critical thinking and digital literacy.** Encourage critical-thinking skills in children by teaching them how to evaluate online information, distinguish between reliable and unreliable sources, and spot misinformation or fake news. Encourage them to question what they see online and think critically about the content they consume.

- **Create tech-free zones and times.** Designate specific areas in your home as tech-free zones, such as the dinner table or bedrooms, to promote face-to-face interaction and reduce screen time. Establish tech-free times, such as before bedtime, to encourage relaxation and healthy sleep habits.

- **Encourage offline activities.** Balance tech usage with offline activities such as outdoor play, arts and crafts, reading books, or engaging in sports and hobbies. Encourage children to explore the world around them, interact with nature, and nurture their creativity through nondigital experiences.

- **Stay informed and engaged.** Stay informed about the latest digital trends, apps, and online platforms that children are using, and engage in regular conversations about their online experiences. Be a supportive and attentive presence in your child's digital life, offering guidance, encouragement, and assurance as they navigate the online world.

Incorporating Healthy Balance

It's important to find the right balance between using technology and spending time doing screen-free activities. Screen-free activities are things you can do without needing to use phones, computers, or tablets.

Importance of Screen-Free Activities

- **Physical health:** engaging in activities such as playing outside, biking, dancing, or playing sports helps keep our bodies healthy.

- **Mental health:** Screen-free activities can help us relax, reduce stress, and improve our focus.

- **Social skills:** Playing with friends in person or spending time with family without screens can help us—especially children—develop important social skills.

Tips for Balancing Technology and Screen-Free Activities

- **Set limits.** It's good to have rules about how much time you can spend using screens each day.

- **Plan screen-free time.** Make a schedule that includes time for screen-free activities such as reading, drawing, playing outside, or doing puzzles.

- **Get creative.** Try out new hobbies or activities that don't involve screens, like gardening, baking, or building things.

- **Plan family time.** Spend quality time with your family by having screen-free meals, playing board games, or going for walks together.

- **Lead by example.** Parents and caregivers can also show kids the importance of balancing technology by being mindful of their own screen time.

Parent Participation

When parents actively participate in their children's tech activities, it can greatly benefit the family dynamic and the kids' overall well-being. Here's a deeper look into the importance of parental involvement in tech activities and understanding parental monitoring and controls:

Building Strong Connections

By participating in tech activities alongside their kids, parents can strengthen their bond and create lasting memories. Whether it's playing a video game, watching a movie, or exploring educational apps together, this shared experience can be a valuable way for families to connect and spend quality time with one another.

Promoting Safe Online Behavior

Understanding how parental controls work allows parents to create a safe and secure online environment for their children. Parental monitoring tools help ensure that kids are protected from inappropriate content and online threats, allowing parents to guide their children's online experiences and teach them responsible digital citizenship.

Fostering Learning and Collaboration

Engaging with children in tech activities provides an opportunity for collaborative learning. Parents can embrace the chance to acquire new tech skills from their kids and, in turn, share their knowledge about responsible tech use. This mutual exchange encourages open communication and establishes a supportive environment for learning and growth.

Empowering Digital Literacy

By being actively involved in their children's tech interactions, parents can empower their kids to become digitally literate. They can ask questions about the tech tools their kids use, demonstrate interest in their online experiences, and promote safe and mindful tech usage through open dialogue and guidance.

Setting Healthy Boundaries and Tech Use

Parents can use their understanding of parental controls to set limits on screen time, manage age-appropriate content, and regulate the use of devices. By having insight into these controls, parents can cultivate a healthy balance between tech use and other activities, instilling the importance of moderation and responsible screen time management in their children.

Screen or Tech Time: Striking a Balance

It's important for kids to strike a balance between screen time and engaging in other activities that promote physical, social, and cognitive development. By incorporating technology into their routines while also participating in offline activities, children can enjoy a well-rounded, enriching experience. Let's explore a few ways technology can captivate kids.

Nature Exploration With Augmented Reality (AR) Apps

Augmented reality (AR) apps offer a unique and interactive way for children to explore the natural world around them. By combining digital elements with real-world environments, AR apps can enhance kids' learning experiences and build curiosity and environmental awareness.

Recommended AR Apps for Identifying Plants and Animals

- **Seek by iNaturalist:** This app allows kids to identify plants and animals by simply pointing their device's camera at them. It provides detailed information about various species, making it a valuable tool for nature enthusiasts.

- **Flora Incognita:** Ideal for plant identification, this AR app helps kids learn about various plant species by analyzing photos taken with their device.

How to Use AR Apps on Hikes or Nature Walks

- **Prepare ahead.** Before heading out on a hike or nature walk, download the AR apps and ensure your device is fully charged.

- **Engage in exploration.** Encourage kids to use the AR apps to identify plants, animals, and other natural elements they encounter along the way. Discuss the information provided by the apps to deepen their understanding of the environment.

- **Capture memories.** Take photos or screenshots of the AR experiences to create a digital nature journal or scrapbook to revisit the learning moments later.

- **Promote discussions about what you've seen.** Use the AR app discoveries as conversation starters to spark curiosity and encourage kids to ask questions about the flora and fauna they encounter.

Encouraging Curiosity and Environmental Awareness

Exploring nature with AR apps not only ignites children's curiosity but also [helps them develop a sense of environmental awareness and appreciation for the world around them. By leveraging technology to enhance their outdoor experiences, kids can develop a deeper connection to nature and cultivate a passion for conservation and sustainability.

Incorporating AR apps into nature exploration activities can inspire a love for the natural world and empower kids to become stewards of the environment. By seamlessly blending technology with outdoor adventures, children can enjoy the best of both worlds and embark on exciting learning journeys that nurture their curiosity and environmental consciousness.

Creative Tech Projects

Introducing children to creative tech projects can be a stimulating and educational way to spark their imagination, hone their skills, and foster a passion for digital creativity. From photography and video-making to exploring different editing tools, these projects offer kids an avenue to express themselves and showcase their talents. Here are a few fun ideas for kids.

Photography and Video-Making

Photography and video-making are fantastic creative tech projects that allow kids to capture moments, tell stories, and unleash their artistic potential. With the accessibility of smartphones and tablets, children can easily dive in and unleash their creativity.

Basic Photography Tips for Kids Using Smartphones or Tablets

- **Focus on composition.** Teach kids about composition basics, such as the rule of thirds and framing, to help them capture visually appealing photos.

- **Experiment with angles.** Encourage kids to explore different angles and perspectives when taking photos to add variety and interest to their shots.

- **Use natural light.** Show kids how to utilize natural light for better photo quality and help them understand the effects of lighting on their photographs.

- **Tell a story.** Encourage children to think about the story they want to convey through their photos and guide them in capturing images that communicate their message.

Fun Video Project Ideas

- **Nature documentaries:** Have kids create their own nature documentaries by filming and narrating scenes from their outdoor adventures.

- **Family interviews:** Encourage children to interview family members and document their responses in a video format, creating a personal and meaningful keepsake.

- **Stop motion animation:** Introduce kids to the world of stop motion animation, where they can bring inanimate objects to life through a series of images.

Simple Editing Apps for Children

- **iMovie:** This user-friendly app allows kids to edit videos easily and add effects, titles, and soundtracks to enhance their creations.

- **Adobe Spark Video:** With this app, children can create engaging video stories by incorporating photos, videos, and voiceovers to produce professional-looking results.

- **Snapseed:** A photo-editing app that offers various tools and filters, Snapseed is great for kids to enhance their photos and unleash their creativity.

Digital Art and Animation

These are also creative methods of expressing ideas and storytelling using technology. Digital art involves creating visual artwork using digital tools like drawing tablets, software programs, and apps, while animation involves bringing drawings, characters, and objects to life through moving images. It's an exciting and fun way for kids to explore their creativity and imagination.

Kid-Friendly Digital Art Tools and Apps

There are so many fun, easy-to-use digital art tools and apps that are perfect for kids. Some popular options include:

- **Drawing apps:** Procreate, Adobe Fresco, and Autodesk SketchBook, among others, provide a wide range of digital brushes and tools for creating amazing artwork.

- **Coloring apps:** Coloring apps such as Recolor and Pigment allow kids to digitally color in and customize pre-drawn artwork.

- **Animation apps:** FlipaClip and Toontastic 3D offer simple, user-friendly interfaces for creating animated stories and characters.

These tools and apps are designed with kids in mind, featuring intuitive controls and engaging interfaces to make the creative process enjoyable and accessible.

Simple Animation Projects Using Scratch

Scratch is a fantastic platform for introducing kids to animation. It's a free programming language and online community where children can program and share their interactive stories, games, and animations. With Scratch, kids can create simple animated stories by programming characters to move, talk, and interact with one another. The drag-and-drop coding blocks make it easy for kids to get started with animation projects and learn basic programming concepts in a fun and interactive way.

Sharing Artwork and Animations Safely Online

When sharing artwork and animations online, kids need to understand how to do so safely and responsibly. Parents should guide them on the importance of privacy and online etiquette. Kids can safely share their creations on platforms like Scratch, where there is a supportive and moderated community, as well as through family-friendly social media platforms and websites where parental controls are in place.

Encouraging kids to explore digital art and animation not only improves fosters their creativity but also introduces them to valuable digital skills that can be useful in the future. Letting them express themselves through technology in a safe and supportive environment can be a rewarding and enriching experience.

Virtual Field Trips and Museum Tours

Virtual tours offer an exciting way for kids to explore and learn about different places, cultures, and historical events without leaving their homes. Through these virtual experiences, kids can visit world-famous landmarks, museums, and historical sites, encouraging their curiosity and expanding their knowledge.

List of Virtual Tours and Field Trip Resources

Some popular virtual tours and field trip resources for kids include:

- **Google Arts & Culture:** This platform offers virtual tours of famous museums and cultural landmarks around the world, allowing kids to explore art collections and historical artifacts.

- **National Park Virtual Tours:** Websites like the National Park Service and National Geographic provide virtual tours of national parks, offering breathtaking views and educational information about nature and wildlife.

- **Smithsonian National Museum of Natural History:** The Smithsonian's website offers interactive virtual tours, enabling kids to discover exhibits on dinosaurs, animals, and ancient civilizations.

- **Zoos and aquariums:** Many zoos and aquariums offer live webcams and virtual tours of their facilities, allowing kids to observe animals and marine life in their natural habitats.

Tips for Making Virtual Tours Interactive and Engaging

To make virtual tours more interactive and engaging for kids, consider the following tips:

- **Discussion and reflection:** Encourage kids to discuss what they see during the virtual tour and ask open-ended questions to prompt critical thinking and reflection.

- **Interactive quizzes and challenges:** Create simple quizzes or challenges related to the tour content to keep kids engaged and to reinforce key learning points.

- **Virtual scavenger hunts:** Provide a list of items or facts for kids to find during the virtual tour, turning it into a fun and interactive scavenger hunt.

- **Role-playing and storytelling:** Encourage kids to imagine themselves in the virtual environment and create stories or role-play based on what they see.

Follow-Up Activities to Enhance Learning

After the virtual tour, consider incorporating follow-up activities to enhance learning, such as:

- **Art projects:** Encourage kids to create artwork inspired by the virtual tour, using the subjects or themes they encountered as inspiration.

- **Writing and journaling:** Prompt kids to write a short story, diary entry, or poem based on their virtual tour experience.

- **Research and presentations:** Assign a mini–research project related to the tour content, and have kids present their findings to the family or their classmates.

- **Virtual show-and-tell:** Allow kids to share their favorite parts of the tour with others through a virtual show-and-tell session.

Tech-Based Group Activities

Tech-based group activities provide a fantastic opportunity for kids to collaborate, learn, and have fun while developing valuable digital skills. These activities include joining online coding clubs and workshops, which offer a supportive and interactive environment for kids to explore the exciting world of coding and programming.

Online Coding Clubs and Workshops

Online coding clubs and workshops are virtual communities where kids can connect with like-minded individuals, participate in coding projects, and learn from experienced mentors. These clubs often offer structured lessons, coding challenges, and opportunities for collaboration on coding projects. They provide a supportive environment where kids can develop their coding skills and share their passion for technology.

Finding and Joining Age-Appropriate Coding Clubs

To find age-appropriate coding clubs and workshops, parents and kids can:

- **Research online.** Search for coding clubs specifically designed for kids in their age group. There are numerous websites and platforms that offer curated lists of coding clubs and workshops.

- **Ask for recommendations.** Reach out to teachers, school counselors, or other parents to gather recommendations for reputable coding clubs suitable for kids.

- **Check local tech organizations.** Explore local tech organizations, libraries, or community centers in the area that may offer coding clubs or workshops for kids.

Benefits of Learning Coding and Programming

Learning coding and programming provides numerous benefits for kids, including:

- **Problem-solving skills:** Coding encourages kids to think logically, break down complex problems into smaller parts, and develop innovative solutions.

- **Creativity and imagination:** Programming allows kids to unleash their creativity by designing and building their own digital creations.

- **Collaboration and communication:** Working on coding projects in groups teaches kids how to collaborate effectively, share ideas, and communicate their thoughts clearly.

- **Digital literacy and future job opportunities:** Learning to code equips kids with important digital literacy skills that are becoming increasingly essential in today's technology-driven world. It also opens up potential career paths in technology fields.

Highlighting Success Stories of Young Coders

There are numerous success stories of young coders who have achieved incredible things. Some notable examples include the following:

- **Emma Yang:** At the age of 14, Emma developed an app called Timeless, designed to help Alzheimer's patients remember people and events.

- **Samaira Mehta:** Samaira started coding at the age of 6 and created a board game called CoderBunnyz to teach others how to code. Now a teenager, she has since become a renowned coder and entrepreneur.

- **Tanmay Bakshi:** Tanmay started coding at the age of 5 and became an expert in artificial intelligence. He has published books and delivered TED Talks about coding and technology.

Multiplayer Educational Games

Multiplayer educational games offer a fun and interactive way for kids to learn and collaborate with others in a virtual environment. These games provide a safe platform for kids to engage in educational activities while building teamwork, communication skills, and critical thinking.

Overview of Safe and Educational Multiplayer Games

Safe and educational multiplayer games are designed to provide a positive and enriching gaming experience for kids. These games often include elements of learning, problem-solving, and skill-building, making them an engaging way to reinforce academic concepts and develop cognitive abilities. Puzzles, quizzes, virtual simulations, and teamwork challenges are examples of such games.

Setting Up Game Time Schedules and Limits

When incorporating multiplayer educational games into a child's routine, it's important to establish game time schedules and limits to ensure a balanced and healthy gaming experience. Parents and caregivers can do the following:

- **Create a game schedule.** Allocate specific times during the day or week for playing educational games, incorporating them into the child's routine alongside other activities.

- **Set time limits.** Limit the duration of gaming sessions to ensure that children have time for other important activities, such as homework, outdoor play, or family time.

- **Monitor and supervise them.** Keep an eye on the child's gaming habits to ensure they are following the established schedule and limits. Provide guidance on balancing gaming with other responsibilities.

Encouraging Teamwork and Communication Through Gaming

Multiplayer educational games present an excellent opportunity for kids to develop teamwork and communication skills while gaming. To encourage these skills, parents and educators can:

- **Emphasize collaboration.** Encourage kids to work together with other players to solve challenges, complete missions, or achieve common goals within the game.

- **Promote communication.** Teach kids the importance of clear communication with teammates, such as sharing information, giving instructions, and listening to others' input.

- **Discuss strategies and problem-solving.** Engage kids in discussions about effective strategies and problem-solving approaches that can be applied both in the game and in real-life situations.

Physical Activities With Tech Integration

Physical activity and exercise are essential for keeping our bodies healthy and strong. In today's world, technology plays a big role in helping us stay active and fit. There are many fun and exciting ways to incorporate technology into physical activities, making exercise more enjoyable for kids and families.

Fitness and Dance Apps

Fitness apps are like personal trainers on your phone or tablet. They can guide you through workouts, track your progress, and even provide motivation and tips. For kids, there are many fitness apps available that are designed to be fun and engaging. These apps often include exercises and challenges that are tailored to children's interests and abilities, making it easier for them to stay active.

Dance apps are another great way to get moving and have fun at the same time. These apps teach kids different dance moves and routines, allowing them to groove to their favorite music while getting a good workout. Whether it's hip-hop, ballet, or just freestyle dancing, there is a dance app out there for everyone.

Fun Fitness Apps and Games

There are also plenty of fitness games available that can turn exercise into a fun, interactive experience. These games often use motion sensors or virtual reality technology to track movement and provide feedback. Kids can play games that involve running, jumping, or even dancing, all while getting a good workout.

Some popular fitness games for kids include virtual reality games that simulate sports like tennis or boxing, as well as games that encourage kids to compete with friends or family members in physical challenges. These games not only promote physical activity but also help kids develop coordination, balance, and strength.

Dance and Movement Apps for Kids

Dance and movement apps are a great way to get kids up and moving. These apps often feature catchy music and easy-to-follow dances that can be done right at home. Kids can learn new dance routines, improve their coordination, and have a blast dancing with their friends or family.

Many dance apps also include interactive features that allow kids to customize dance routines or even create choreography. This not only encourages creativity but also helps kids build confidence in their dancing abilities.

Creating a Family Fitness Challenge

One fun way to incorporate technology into physical activities is by creating a family fitness challenge using tech devices. Family members can set goals, track their progress, and compete with each other in various fitness challenges. This can be a great way to motivate each other, stay accountable, and spend quality time together.

For example, everyone in the family can use fitness trackers or apps to log their daily steps, set workout goals, or compete in virtual challenges. By making fitness a family affair, parents can lead by example and instill healthy habits in their children from a young age.

Outdoor Sports With Tech Gadgets

Outdoor sports are a fantastic way for kids to stay active, have fun, and enjoy the great outdoors. With the help of modern technology, there are plenty of gadgets and devices that can make the experience even more exciting and rewarding.

Using Pedometers and Fitness Trackers to Set Goals

Pedometers and fitness trackers are wearable devices that can count your steps, measure your heart rate, and track your physical activity throughout the day. These devices can be especially helpful for kids who want to set goals and monitor their progress.

Kids can use pedometers to challenge themselves to take more steps each day; fitness trackers can help them keep track of their workouts and activity levels. This can be a great way to encourage kids to be more mindful of their physical activity and lead a healthier lifestyle.

Beginner-Friendly Sports Tech

Beginner-friendly sports tech refers to gadgets and equipment that are designed to help kids learn and improve their skills in a particular sport. For example, there are smart soccer balls that have sensors inside them, allowing kids to measure things like kick speed, accuracy, and distance.

These smart soccer balls can provide valuable feedback to young players, helping them identify areas for improvement and track their progress over time. Similar technologies exist for other sports, as well, such as basketballs and baseball gloves with built-in sensors.

Tracking Progress and Celebrating Milestones

One of the most exciting aspects of using sports tech gadgets is the ability to track progress and celebrate milestones. By using these devices, kids can see how their skills and abilities improve over time, providing a great sense of achievement and motivation.

For example, kids can track the distance they run or cycle, the number of goals they score, or the speed of their kicks. With this data, they can set personal records, beat their own best performances, and celebrate their accomplishments. This can be incredibly empowering and encouraging for young athletes.

Mindful Tech Usage

Mindful tech usage involves being aware of screen time, setting limits, and balancing technology with other activities that promote well-being. By implementing strategies for mindful tech usage, kids can maintain a healthy relationship with technology and prioritize other important aspects of their lives.

Setting Screen Time Limits

Setting screen time limits is a crucial component of mindful tech usage for kids. Parents can establish guidelines and rules around how much time children are allowed to spend on devices each day. By setting clear boundaries, kids can develop a healthy balance between screen time and other activities such as outdoor play, reading, or spending time with family and friends.

Recommended Screen Time Guidelines for Different Ages

It's essential to consider age-appropriate screen time guidelines when regulating children's tech usage. The American Academy of Pediatrics recommends the following general guidelines for screen time:

- **For children under 18 months:** Avoid the use of screens, except for video chatting.

- **For children aged 18–24 months:** Limit screen time to high-quality programming, and co-viewing with a caregiver.

- **For children aged 2–5 years:** Limit screen time to 1 hour per day of high-quality programming.

- **For children aged 6 years and older:** Establish consistent limits on screen time and ensure it does not interfere with sleep, physical activity, or other healthy behaviors.

Tools and Apps for Managing and Monitoring Screen Time

Various tools and apps are available to help parents manage and monitor their children's screen time. Parental control features on devices, apps, and software solutions allow parents to set time limits, restrict access to certain apps or websites, and monitor usage patterns. These tools can provide valuable insights into how much time kids are spending on screens and help parents make adjustments as needed.

Some popular apps and tools for managing screen time include Screen Time (available on iOS devices), Family Link (provided by Google), and Qustodio. These tools empower parents to create a healthy tech environment for their children while promoting responsible device usage.

Encouraging Breaks and Nontech Activities

Encouraging breaks from screens and engaging in nontech activities are essential for promoting balance and well-being. Kids should have opportunities to participate in physical activities, hobbies, and social interactions that do not involve technology. Encouraging outdoor play, reading books, creating art, or engaging in sports can help children develop a diverse range of skills and interests beyond their phones and tablets.

Balancing Online and Offline Activities

As we've already seen, spending too much time on screens can have negative effects on physical and mental health. By practicing a healthy balance of online and offline activities, kids can prioritize their well-being and develop a range of diverse interests and skills.

Strategies for Maintaining a Healthy Balance

Maintaining a healthy balance between online and offline activities involves being mindful of how much time is spent on screens and making intentional choices to prioritize offline activities. Strategies for maintaining a healthy balance include:

- Setting limits on screen time

- Scheduling specific times for online activities and offline activities

- Using technology to enhance other activities, such as researching topics related to hobbies or interests

- Taking breaks from screens and engaging in physical activities or outdoor play

- Prioritizing in-person social interactions over online social media interactions

Encouraging Offline Hobbies and Interests

One way to help kids maintain a healthy balance between online and offline activities is to encourage offline hobbies and interests. Parents can help encourage children to explore and develop hobbies, such as reading, drawing, playing an instrument, or engaging in physical activities like sports or dancing. These hobbies can provide a sense of fulfillment and joy outside of screen time.

Family Tech-Free Time Ideas and Routines

Family tech-free time can provide opportunities for families to facilitate in-person interactions and engage in offline activities together. Families can establish tech-free routines, such as device-free dinners or game nights that prioritize in-person social interactions.

Other family tech-free time ideas include:

- Going for a family hike or walk

- Participating in a family game night

- Doing a puzzle together

- Reading books or telling stories aloud together

- Visiting a park, museum, or other outdoor recreational area

As the digital world continues to evolve and provide new opportunities for creativity and learning, it's clear that tuned-in technology has the potential to enhance the way kids experience their summer adventures. From virtual field trips to educational apps, the possibilities are endless when it comes to incorporating technology into summer fun.

As we near the end of this book, we have explored various ways to make summer memorable and enjoyable for kids of all ages. From outdoor adventures to creative crafts, each chapter has offered valuable insights and ideas to create lasting memories during the summer season. Now, let's wrap up our journey together by reflecting on the importance of making the most of these precious moments and keeping the spirit of summer alive all year.

Conclusion

Summer is a time for fun and excitement, and it can be a precious opportunity to spend quality time with your children. Whether you have a few weeks or a few months of summer break, it is crucial to maximize this time to create memories that will last a lifetime. *Summer Fun for Kids* provides an excellent resource for parents seeking creative and engaging activities to explore during this season, both indoors and outdoors.

One of the most important takeaways from this guide is the value of actively involving your children in the planning and execution of summer activities. By giving them a voice in the process, you allow them to invest in the experience, creating a sense of ownership and purpose. This helps to optimize opportunities for bonding and creating memories that can be cherished for years to come.

An essential aspect of making summer memories with your children is to keep detailed notes. As the summer progresses, maintain a log or journal that lists the activities you do, any struggles or successes experienced, and anything that stood out in the experience. This will allow you to reflect back on the summer and create a lasting memory book with your children, in which they can reflect on and share their favorite moments from the summer.

Remember—be adaptable and flexible when it comes to summer activities with your children. As they grow and develop, their interests change, so you'll need to personalize the activities you plan to ensure they remain engaging and relevant. Investing the time and resources needed for making these adaptations can enhance the summer experience and create meaningful shared experiences.

Spending quality time with your family during the summer is vital for establishing strong bonds and creating lasting impressions. Bonding doesn't necessarily require grand gestures. Simple acts, such as going on a family picnic or taking a hike in a nearby park, allows everyone to disconnect from the often-busy schedules of daily life, allowing you to create meaningful memories together.

Don't forget to remind children about the importance of creating a balance between outdoor activities and technology. During the summer, it is easy to fall into the habit of spending too much time indoors and in front of screens. Still, it is crucial to monitor and restrict screen time to ensure that children have enough time to engage in outdoor activities, spend time with loved ones, and explore new passions.

Finally, this book emphasizes that engaging in activity and creativity isn't something that should only happen during the summer months. Looking at all these ideas and activities as year-round possibilities can help sustain the joy of summer throughout the year. By sharing your experiences with others, you can inspire other parents to get creative with their children, further enhancing the joy of the season for all.

By embracing quality time together, remaining adaptable and reflective, focusing on the importance of balance between outdoor activities and technology, and promoting year-round creativity, you can ensure that summer is an exciting and enjoyable time for the whole family.

Share your insights on how the activities have enhanced your family's summer fun. Your reflections and input not only provide valuable guidance for future improvements but also enable you to deepen your understanding of the impact of these activities on your family dynamics and connections. It will also help other parents plan ahead for a fun-filled summer with their children. Have fun this summer and cherish the memories with your loved ones. We hope this guide has given you a few ideas to brighten up your kids' vacation.

References

david. (2024, May 10). *Benefits of summer camp activities | summer camps*. Activ Camps. https://www.activcamps.com/2024/05/benefits-of-summer-camp-activities/

Fatima. (2024, April 12). *Fun outdoor summer activities for kids and friends*. VEDANTU. https://www.vedantu.com/blog/fun-outdoor-summer-activities-for-kids-and-friends

Fortin, D. (2021, November 13). *Fun recipes to bake with kids*. Del's Cooking Twist. https://www.delscookingtwist.com/fun-recipes-to-bake-with-kids/

Gautieri, A. & Thomas, M. (2024, April 11). *These cute summer crafts will inspire your kids' creativity*. Good Housekeeping. https://www.goodhousekeeping.com/home/craft-ideas/g20967550/summer-crafts/

How to make a volcano: step-by-step experiment. (2024, January 12). Kiddus. https://kiddus.com/blogs/blog/how-to-make-a-volcano-step-by-step-experiment-simple-and-safe

Incorporating technology into children's activities: pros and cons. Kidztivity. (2023, November 16). Https://Kidztivity.com/. https://kidztivity.com/incorporating-technology-into-childrens-activities/

LaScala, M. (2020, April 20). *The "shaving cream water cycle" experiment is an easy science project you can do With Kids at Home*. Good Housekeeping. https://www.goodhousekeeping.com/life/parenting/g32176446/science-experiments-for-kids/

Learn, S. (2024, May 14). *75 best summer quotes for kids in 2024*. www.splashlearn.com/.

https://www.splashlearn.com/blog/best-summer-quotes-for-kids/#2-15-funny-summer-quotes-for-kids-

Liliana. (2021, August 27). *Family theme days ideas for parents and kids.* Mighty Kids. https://mightykidsacademy.com/top-family-theme-day-ideas-which-will-make-you-want-to-celebrate-every-weekend/

Managing screen time: balancing technology use for children. (2024, May 7). www.totsnteenspediatrics.com. https://www.totsnteenspediatrics.com/blog/1155113-managing-screen-time-balancing-technology-use-for-children

Nicolette. (2023, April 25). *Tips for summer road trips with kids.* How Does She. https://howdoesshe.com/tips-for-summer-road-trips-with-kids/

Sager, J. (2023, January 13). *20 fun indoor recess games that will save the day (and your sanity).* Teach Starter. https://www.teachstarter.com/us/blog/16-fun-indoor-recess-games-that-will-save-the-day-and-your-sanity-2/

Made in United States
Orlando, FL
08 May 2025

61145899R00085